PARIS to PROVENCE

ETHEL BRENNAN & SARA REMINGTON

PARIS *to* PROVENCE

Childhood Memories of Food & France

Photography by Sara Remington   Foreword by Georgeanne Brennan

Andrews McMeel
Publishing, LLC
Kansas City • Sydney • London

Andrews McMeel Publishing, LLC
an Andrews McMeel Universal company
1130 Walnut Street, Kansas City, Missouri 64106
www.andrewsmcmeel.com

13 14 15 16 17 TEN 10 9 8 7 6 5 4 3 2

ISBN: 978-1-4494-2751-1

Library of Congress Control Number: 2012952342

Design: Francesca Bautista
Photography: Sara Remington
Food Stylist: Ethel Brennan
Prop Stylist: Ethel Brennan
Recipe Testing: Abby Stolfo
Recipes: Ethel Brennan
Photo Editing: Imelda Picherit

www.ethelbrennan.com
www.sararemington.com

ATTENTION: SCHOOLS AND BUSINESSES
Andrews McMeel books are available at quantity discounts with bulk purchase for edu-
cational, business, or sales promotional use. For information, please e-mail the Andrews
McMeel Special Sales Department: specialsales@amuniversal.com

Ethel

Paris to Provence is for my beautiful, inquisitive children,
Oscar and Raphael, and for their father: my loving, supportive, creative, and
ever-charming husband, Laurent.

Sara

To my parents, Toni and Bill Remington, the most amazing,
100 percent supportive, fun, all-things-French-loving couple. You are
the reason why I am who I am today, and this book wouldn't exist without you.
You gave Jennifer and me the gift of travel and adventure, the best gift
you can give your kids. Thank you. I am the luckiest daughter in
the whole world. I love you!

Contents

FOREWORD
by Georgeanne Brennan

When I was twenty, I took a motorbus tour of Europe that included the high points of the continent: Amsterdam, Paris, Brussels, Rome, Venice, Florence, Geneva, Heidelberg, Frankfurt, and Innsbruck. I was already in love with the idea of Europe, beginning with my childhood fairy tales set in castles and ancient forests with strange sounding names, then, later, in college, reading European literature and history, and of course, everything by Hemingway and F. Scott Fitzgerald. Once I arrived in Europe, I discovered not only the cobbled streets and centuries-old buildings seeping with history but also the food—especially the food. Inadvertently, food became my touchstone of place. Whether I was in Paris or Venice, Heidelberg or Brussels, I wanted to taste everything. The bakeries enticed me with the scent of their freshly baked breads and rolls, and their artfully arrayed pastries. Delicatessens beckoned to me with their displays of pickled herrings, mysterious-looking sliced meats, mushrooms, and a myriad of vegetables bathed in different sauces. What did they all taste like? Behind the counters of the meat markets stood the butchers, all dressed in white with their sharp knives at the ready, framed by curtains of hanging cured meats and scarred butcher blocks, patiently waiting for their customers' requests. Cheeses were everywhere and none was familiar. Small, soft rounds of cheese sat near more cheeses in big, heavy wheels and large round balls. Some of the larger rounds were covered with red wax, others with yellow, some tattooed with dates and undecipherable signs. A few of the cheeses had wedges cut and removed from them, allowing me just a glimpse of the different interior textures and colors.

Every city had vast open markets full of vendors in stalls selling fruits, vegetables, cheeses, fish, and meats of every description. As if by magic, the markets sprung up in the morning, filling a square and spilling out into the neighboring streets, and—poof!—by lunch they had disappeared. I simply couldn't get my fill of the experience of the food. I had been prepared for the sight of the Seine and the Rhône, the towers of Heidelberg Castle and Notre Dame, for the Piazza San Marco and its bells, for the Michaelangelos, the Eiffel Tower, and the Louvre, but not for the taste of the crusty, fresh roll I bought in Amsterdam, stacked with sweet ham and an unknown cheese, nor for the briny pickled herrings, slathered with cream and onions, that I sampled in Frankfurt, nor for my first bite of a *mille-feuille* in Paris.

I ate my way though the trip, savoring every meal the tour offered, mostly modest, at bistros, *gasthauses*, or *trattorias*, depending upon the country. It was all new. Breakfasts were extraordinary, with hot coffee and hot milk or cream, freshly baked breads, sweet butter, homemade jams, and, if in the north, platters of cheeses, meats, and smoked fish. Pastas with thick meat sauces, liver and onions, thin steaks with heaps of *pommes frites*, rich stews, salads dressed only with unctuous olive oil and wine vinegar, cheeses and more cheese, cakes, custards—I ate it all and with each bite fell deeper in love with the Old World. Each place in my maiden voyage became marked in my memory by the aromas and flavors I had encountered there.

At the end of that summer, as I was preparing for my junior-year abroad study program, I was assigned an apartment in Aix-en-Provence, where I lived with a roommate from Chicago who loved food and cooking as much as I did. However, I was far more interested in shopping at the daily open market and cooking on our two-burner hot plate than I was in going to classes. As planned, Donald, my California boyfriend, came to visit, but unplanned, we got married in late November in the *Salle de Mariage* in Aix. We headed to West Berlin, he to study German and work on his master's degree, and I, ostensibly, to write and paint, but above all, to shop and to cook. Every morning for months, I set out to visit my neighborhood bakeries, butcher shops, cheese stores, and markets, bringing home fresh discoveries to cook. With my husband, I foraged the city's beer houses to discover their rustic fare. When spring came we went south to Greece and Spain where I reveled in the food of the Mediterranean before returning to California.

When, not too many years later, Donald and I decided to return to Europe, this time to buy a farmhouse and raise goats in Provence, I was elated and apprehensive as well. We moved there with our two-year-old daughter, Ethel, our dog, and all our belongings, which for me included not only my cookbooks, dishes, silver, pots and pans, linens, tools and everything else but my childhood memorabilia of books, paper dolls, scrapbooks, even prom dresses, plus my grandmother's china, cast-iron skillet, and my mother's Revere Ware, Le Creuset, and recipe box. I saw my life as a continuum linked by food and cooking.

As I learned to take care of goats and to make goats' milk cheese, so did Ethel. She was my constant companion, becoming adept at milking the goats, hand turning our soft cheeses, and even herding our pig to the abandoned pear trees to eat the fallen fruit. Together, Ethel and I found our first wild mushrooms—chanterelles and cèpes—in the neighboring forest in fall, spotted the spears of wild asparagus in spring, made simple sausage, and stirred simmering vegetable soups atop our wood-burning stove.

Although two and half years later our family left Provence to return to California, now with a new baby brother for Ethel, our high school teaching jobs allowed us to return, every summer, to our little farm in Provence, each trip punctuated by visits to somewhere special—Rhine River castles, the French Basque country, the Italian coast, and always Paris, and always a small car.

"Mom, Mom, you won't believe this! I'm working with a photographer who had the exact childhood I did, going to France every summer with her sister and her parents, driving all over in a little car and going swimming all the time, just like we did! And, she remembers all the same food I do—the *beignets*, and *poulet frites*, and ice creams, and late-night dinners, and everything!" It was Ethel on the phone. I could hear not only the excitement in her voice but her passion for food, not just how it tastes or looks but how it resonates to bring back to life a place and time in her memory. And now, she'd found someone else who understood and shared that with her—Sara Remington.

Sara stayed with me in Provence one fall for a week, as part of a larger trip she was making to France. She wanted to see where Ethel had spent her childhood summers—the lakes, villages, fields, and forests of the Haut Var, Alpes d'Haute Provence, and of course, Nice and the Mediterranean beaches. I filled my tiny kitchen with the foods of memory that Sara talked about—jams, Nutella, slabs of sweet butter, bars of rich chocolate. Every evening, after her adventures, I cooked dinner for us—roast chicken with wild thyme, thick soups to eat along with fresh baguettes, even one night a guinea fowl with mushrooms and cabbage. As we lingered over our wine, I listened to her memories of her childhood summers spent in France, and how much they meant to her then and now. I thought to myself how gratifying it must be for her parents, as it is for me, to have played a part in passing on to our daughters a passion for food and place.

In this book, *Paris to Provence*, Ethel and Sara have captured their collective memories in images, text, and recipes, bringing their childhood back to life, and in so doing, speak to all of us, remind us all of our own memories of food and place, regardless of how simple or how grand the places and food might have been. Through their book, they remind us to reflect upon what food means to children and families, and how important it is to share that time together when memories and enduring values are formed. As I watch my young grandsons, Ethel's children, picking the asparagus from my garden, roasting the spears with me, then eating them at the table with us, their extended family, I think that maybe the gene for love of food and family must have been passed on to yet another generation, which is what *Paris to Provence* celebrates.

INTRODUCTION

As children we experience the world around us with wonder and amazement, using all of our senses. For Sara and me, France embodies the visual, tactile, and romantic personal histories we have carefully and thoughtfully carried into adulthood. Our memories are filled with images of old, faded, and peeling advertisements painted on the crumbling plaster walls of buildings, hand-shaped brass door knockers, saggy beds in slightly suspect hotels, crisp vintage linens with hand-stitched monograms, tiny Paris elevators with polished nickel doors, and the pale, pink light of summer evenings settling over vineyards and fields of wheat. The sounds of our childhood are as powerful, if not more so, than the visual memories. Squeaky wood floors from the eighteenth century, church bells every hour of the day, children's voices in Luxembourg Gardens floating through the late afternoon air, the soft, melodic whine of police and ambulance sirens echoing off the ancient walls, heavy steel *pétanque* balls colliding and clacking—all have left us with illustrated vignettes of our childhood.

Although we are ten years apart in age and have only become friends in the last several years, we share the unusual experience of having been American children in France. The common thread is our memories of food and place, whether gently unwrapping sugar cubes from papers and dipping them into our parents' coffee at the café, or diving into the warm Mediterranean sea from the rocky *calanques* near Marseille to get an ice cream from the boat vendor. *Paris to Provence* is the story of two young girls discovering the beauty and wonder of how food, landscape, and travel are inseparable from our memories and experiences. The raw and unpretentious connection the French seemingly have to food, place, and each other is now part of our adult lives. The following stories, each narrated by us individually, reflect our unique memories, but through overlap and shared experiences here is a collective history of the food we discovered, places we visited, and people we knew.

ETHEL

The age difference between me and Sara at certain times seems like a generation and at other times insignificant. Sara and I grew up on opposite sides of the country, me in northern California and she in upstate New York, but strangely enough, we have a shared past, not a physical one, but an overlapping one. Our parents are not friends or even acquaintances, but were inspired travelers. They were drawn to France, where consequently, Sara and I spent many of our childhood summers, though not together or even in the same decade. After our first time working together as photographer and stylist, Sara and I quickly realized we had both spent our childhood summers piled into the backseats of tiny French cars, she with her older sister and I with my younger brother, traveling the small, winding country roads through terraced vineyards, lavender fields, and cherry orchards. Some years my family would begin our summer adventure in Paris, other times in London, taking the English Channel ferries to Calais or Ostend in Belgium.

My French life began in 1971, when my parents, graduate students in California, packed up their bohemian student life in La Jolla, California, along with me and our dog, and moved to France to raise goats and make cheese. Dreams of another life, a bucolic life very removed from the American residue of the staid and stifled 1950s and the trauma of the Vietnam War, are partly what brought my parents to France. They bought a farmhouse in the inner Var, a remote region of Provence once called "*le pays perdu*," the lost country, because of its inaccessibility by train, airport, or highway. This became my childhood home.

I know their story, and even though I am not sure if the memories are mine or if they are family stories told over the years, they have become interwoven and inseparable from my own memories. However, my story begins at age three with roasted chestnuts and ultimately winds through my childhood and early teens, which I spent between Provence and northern California. The mix was unusual to say the least. I had my American life and I had my French life, and they seemed more often than not to collide with the subject of food.

The fall I turned two years old, shortly before we moved to France, my mother and I had traveled to New York, staying with Sondra Leftoff, a lifelong friend of my mother and now of mine. On that trip we bought roasted chestnuts wrapped in newspaper cones from street vendors in Manhattan. Our next stop was Paris, where we again had roasted chestnuts bought on the street. Once my family moved back to California, I don't believe I ever had roasted chestnuts again until I graduated from college and made them myself. They exploded in the oven during a dinner party because I did not know to score the thick woody skins to allow the built-up steam to escape.

Although my family only lived a little more than two years in Provence with the goats and making cheese before returning to California where my parents became high school teachers, we returned every summer to our old stone farmhouse, leaving as soon as school got out, traveling there by various routes, and once settled in, exploring our world with day trips to the sea, to lakes, and to neighboring villages and castles. It was there, during those long, lazy summers with my family, that I learned the smells of the forest as we gathered wild herbs, the taste of truly fresh fish and vegetables, and the pleasure of lingering over the table.

Thus began my journey from Paris to Provence, starting and ending in Paris. I now visit my French in-laws who live in Paris, and in between, I share those long drives to Provence with my husband and twin boys, in a larger car, but still to visit my childhood home and friends.

SARA

Every other year in May, before my sister and I finished school, my parents would map out a different route through France, snaking our way through big cities and small towns. Some routes were determined by the availability of friends for our visit, others were determined by adventure, but no two routes were the same. A typical summertime journey would start in Paris, then swing over to the west to Rennes, include a little jaunt up to Saint Malo, then wind down to Bordeaux, then over to Lyon where my father went to medical school (and where my mom drove every weekend from Paris to visit him before they were married), on to Geneva, and would always end up in Provence. This is the reason why Paris and Provence memories are the strongest for me: our constant starting point and ending point.

We began these adventures in the early 1980s when I was three years old and my sister was four. What originally brought my parents to France wasn't a change of pace or lifestyle, but because my dad had attended medical school in Lyon years earlier. They had always shared a connection to the people, the wine, the food, and French culture, and in turn, wanted my sister and me to experience some of the same adventures they had had in their late twenties and early thirties. Now that I am that same age at what I'm sure seemed to them a time of "endless possibilities of love, life, and travel," I too am experiencing the pangs of French wanderlust. When I visit France today, I feel like I've arrived at my second home, and I want to eat and drink my way through the streets of Paris, the wineries of Bordeaux, and the markets of Provence.

In this book are the sounds, the smells, the textures, and the tastes of my childhood summertime—picnics on the Seine with cheese and wine; late family hours-long dinners with course after delicious course (even though my sister and I were impatient and so badly wanted to get up from the table); white ham or *jambon cru* with butter on a cream-colored, soft, and crispy baguette; *goûter* (a simple snack of baguette and chocolate) after swimming in the Mediterranean for hours; roasted chestnuts and crepes with butter and sugar on a Paris street corner; picking blackberries in endless green fields with French friends (then eating them in secret tree houses!). Memories like these are some of the reasons why I am a photographer to this day. I was pleasantly surprised to learn that Ethel experienced a very similar way of life during her childhood summers as well, and with these words, recipes, images, and journals, we reminisce what a luscious childhood our parents created for us.

To leave one's home as a child and visit a foreign country forms impressions embedded for a lifetime. These memories are most often shared with siblings and parents who traveled together, but Sara and I discovered that we each understood practically down to the sauce on the meat and the faces of the elderly women who pinched our cheeks what the other had experienced in France. As children, we were different because no one else in our schools or on our blocks had traveled to France in the summers and eaten exotic foods such as snails, tiny fried fish, rich cakes, and salted hams. Ours were solitary experiences, ones not really made for sharing in the early days of September once back to school but for keeping to ourselves. Now years later, we are enchanted by our own childhoods, continually folding so much of what we experienced into our contemporary lives.

The recipes are the outline of the natural progression of our summer holidays, which began with the first steps off the plane, tumbled into long road travels to the south of France, stopped at open-air *marchés*, and followed by picnics, wanderings through ancient villages, and swims in the tepid Mediterranean Sea. As the days went on and we settled with friends and families, meals and drinks were shared in cafés, afternoon *goûter* with local children, and last, but possibly most cherished, long lazy meals with family and friends. The recipes were selected as bookmarks for our memories: individual ham and cheese quiches purchased at a bakery the morning of a long stretch of driving, oven-roasted tomatoes purchased from open markets abundant in the flush of summer, and always, at least once, butter- and garlic-drenched snails.

Chapter 1
PARIS TO PROVENCE,
THE ROAD TRIP

Cornichon Pickles

Pâté de Campagne
Rustic Country Pâté

Pissaladière
Onion Tart

Pizza aux Anchois et Olives Noires
Pizza with Anchovies and Black Olives

Poulet Rôti avec Pommes de Terre
Rotisserie Chicken with Potatoes

Steak au Poivre à la Sauce aux Morilles
Pepper Steak with Morels

Sandwiches Jambon Crudités
Ham and Crudités Sandwiches

Quiche Lorraine

Tarte aux Pommes
Apple and Custard Tart

Tarte Tropézienne
Brioche Tart with Crème Pâtisserie

The drive from Paris to Provence marks the beginning of our story.
It is on this stretch of the vacation that we muddled through jet lag and headed to the bakeries, cafés, shops, and markets to rediscover our beloved candies, pastries, sandwiches, and drinks. For this reason, many of the recipes are interchangeable within various chapters, but decisions had to be made, and for us, the following foods, such as tiny cornichon pickles, salty squares of black olive and anchovy pizza, truck-stop prix fixe menus of *steak au poivre*, cheese, decadent cream-filled *pâtisseries*, and sandwiches filled with ham, butter, salt-cured meats, and liver-rich pâté mark the beginning of summers spent in France.

The journey from Paris to the South now can be done in three hours by TGV, but during the 1970s and 1980s the fast trains were not yet a fixture in the European commute, and long, slow car trips were the way we traveled. The standard car rental was the now classic Renault 4, small and boxy with scratchy, ruglike upholstery, a tight fit for our family of four, luggage for two months, and often a small dog. My younger brother Oliver and I filled the backseat with toys, books, drawing pads, and snacks, an imaginary line drawn down the center of the blue and red woven seat in an effort to keep the bickering to a minimum. Usually the trip would take several days, beginning with a short stay in a borrowed Paris apartment, often a seven-floor walk-up, the twisting stairwell filled with the lingering smells of waxed tiles, musty wood, and sautéed onions. Once at the top, settled in for the night, the city sounds of sirens, people, and honking horns, mixed with a dose of jet lag, would keep me awake, my sleeplessness fueled by the excitement of the coming weeks. Days in Paris were spent wandering the streets, exploring the creepy catacombs and ancient cemeteries, a must-do every year, visiting any museums or churches missed in previous years, and, of course, eating.

Leaving Paris was a predawn tradition, with my father frantically trying to get out of the city before the chaos of traffic would leave us trapped in the roundabout circling the Arc de Triomphe. Each summer, although the start and end points were the same, the map took us through the winding landscapes of France, my forehead leaning against the car window as I daydreamed of what life might have been like hundreds of years earlier in the endless stream of castles perched on hillsides and cliffs we passed. Each truck stop held the promise of shops filled with magical European toys and unheard-of regional delicacies like jarred *pied-paquet* (lamb's feet and tripe), cans of snails topped with a cylinder of shells to stuff them into, and condiments of every kind, packaged in toothpaste-style tubes: mayonnaise, *harissa*, mustard, chestnut cream, and sweetened condensed milk. Next stop, a walk over the *autoroute*, or freeway, in elevated passageways to the cafeteria, comparable to a three-star restaurant back in the States. A not-so-quick, sit-down lunch of braised endive in cream sauce, grilled steak au poivre, and wine for the grown-ups, sweet, caramel-drenched flan, and then strong espresso-style coffees, also for grown-ups. During coffee time, my brother and I would escape the table and wind our way back to the shops and plan our pitch for a new toy or candy, preferably both.

Once on the road, each night guaranteed a different hotel, but all seemed to have saggy mattresses and chenille bedspreads. In the mornings, without fail, we would be served a

glorious breakfast of fresh, warm croissants, jam, and rich, creamy hot chocolate before heading out for new adventures, some more memorable than others. One such was the time we arrived after dark in the village of Mont Saint-Michel, an ancient, Gothic abbey built on a rocky island, which rises from the low tides practically in the middle of the ocean. Required to park outside the walls, we set off into the village to find a hotel, and when we returned several hours later for our luggage, after a yummy dinner finished with three scoops of ice cream, topped with a mountain of crème Chantilly, the car had been broken into and our backpacks of toys stolen. Although sad, all was quickly forgotten by assurances of new toys to be found in the next village or truck stop.

Another year, all the way at the other end of France, a trip over the Alps was lengthened by what might have been hours or days by the *transhumance*, a now nearly extinct practice of walking herds of sheep and goats from the hot dry hills of Provence to the cooler, grassy mountains of the Alps, an arduous trek for the shepherd and his herd and a road hazard for car travelers such as us. I remember very clearly hanging out the window as hundreds of very smelly goats and sheep surrounded our car, which was stopped in the middle of the road, on one side the high mountain wall, on the other a very long and steep cliff. Thankfully we had plenty of snacks, bottles of Evian, dry salami, a bag of fresh baked madeleines, bread, and, most likely, several fresh goat cheeses.

—Ethel

As a kid, I thought if I flapped my arms really hard, I would be able to fly, just barely floating above the ground. I envisioned this as my own little dream road trip sans car, slow and methodical, experiencing sights and colors from an angle that no one else would be able to touch. I continued to have this daydream summer after summer in France, from the backseat of a tiny cheap rental car. Looking out the backseat car window was almost as good as the idea of being a human bird—I had my imagination as my silent playground as I tried to follow each blade of grass flying by, my fingers touching the green tips in the endless fields.

The weeks and days leading up to the road trip were so fun. My parents, for the most part, would have the same routine, visit the same friends, with slight differences in course. There was comfort in familiarity, comfort in routine and tradition, knowing what was going to happen next in a general sense, but the details would fill themselves out later. As kids, we were oblivious to the conversations about mapping our route. The trips just magically happened.

Strangely enough, the smell of diesel fuel that always struck my nostrils so abruptly as we entered smoggy Paris was a comfort. The smell reminded me of movement, progress, and adventure. We would arrive at the one-star hotel where we always stayed, Hôtel de la Paix (now out of business), and knew what we were getting into. After about the fourth visit, the little old lady who owned the hotel would stand up from behind the counter with excitement, a huge smile taking over her wrinkles with more wrinkles, speaking mumbled French where I would catch every other word at most. Much of the banter was "*Oh la la les filles, elles sont très belles et grandes! Oh la la la la!*" and this was always followed by a giant, wet kiss that left me smiling but cringing, running to the other room to wipe my cheek without her seeing. I still remember that noise of the old woman at the hotel kissing my cheek: much like the sound of a cork being slowly pulled out of a wine bottle, ending with a pop!

We always had a room on one of the top floors with no elevator, but my dad would gladly haul all of our suitcases up the narrow winding staircase. The sag of the hotel bed and the sound of the old bedsprings as we plopped our suitcases on top of the mattresses felt like old friends. The bathroom down the hall, window knobs that squeaked as you opened them to let the sounds of Paris into our tiny rooms, the peeling paint on the ceiling: all were there to remind us that we'd begun our adventure.

—Sara

CORNICHON PICKLES

As all kids do, I loved, and still love, anything miniature. Small meant playful, playful meant fun, fun was supposed to go along with everything we ate. It was as though we were playing house as we were eating miniature things, as if we were giants in control of our tiny food. The same goes for the tiny, salty white onions that cornichons are traditionally pickled with—they repulsed and fascinated me by how much they reminded me of eyeballs. When I opened a jar and looked inside, I would see faces looking up at me—the tiny onions were the eyes, the peppercorns were the pupils, and the cornichons were smiles or frowns, depending on how they lay under the onions. My mom told me that she first had these when she was a student in Paris and thought they were so elegant—a treat, miniature salty delights. We would devour the mini pickles in a glass bowl served beside the raclette cheese and pâtés, always waiting for us as we arrived at a friend's house.

—Sara

2 pounds small pickling cucumbers,
  such as gherkins
2 (1-pint) glass canning jars, lids, and rings,
  such as Kerr
2 cups distilled white vinegar
2 cups of water
¼ cup pickling salt

6 pearl onions, peeled
1 clove garlic, peeled and halved
3 sprigs fresh dill
1 teaspoon black peppercorns
1 teaspoon whole mustard seeds
2 fresh or dried bay leaves

To ensure crisp pickles, rehydrate them by placing the cucumbers in a bowl of water, uncovered, and let stand overnight at room temperature.

Bring a large pot of water to a boil, then gently lower the jars, lids, and rings into the pot and boil for 15 minutes to sterilize. It is best to have the jars hot right before filling them. Reserve the water.

In a medium saucepan, bring the vinegar, 2 cups water, and salt to a boil over high heat.

Divide the onions, garlic, fresh dill, peppercorns, mustard seeds, and bay leaves between the two sterilized jars. Drain the cucumbers from the soaking water and pack into the jars, leaving ½-inch headspace from the top of the jars. Fill the jars with the hot vinegar mixture, leaving ¼-inch headspace from the top of the jar, and fit the lids and rings. Return the pot of water to a boil, place the jars upright in the boiling water, and process for 15 minutes. Remove from the pot and let stand for 24 hours. Store in a cool, dark place for 3 to 4 weeks before opening. Alternatively, let the jars cool once filled and refrigerate for up to one month.

makes 2 (1-pint) jars

PÂTÉ DE CAMPAGNE
Rustic Country Pâté

Pâté was a daily treat for us in France and an occasional weekend treat at home. Whenever there were guests present in the Remington house in upstate New York, we had a plate of cornichons, mustard, and Pâté de Campagne. The Triscuits—those pedestrian salty square baked wafers found in every U.S. supermarket—we paired with the pâté were a bit of a lowbrow toast to our French adventures. I still love them, no matter how processed they are. They're part of my Pâté de Campagne memory.

—Sara

1 tablespoon Cognac

¼ pound pork liver, finely chopped

1 pound pork butt, finely chopped

¼ pound fatback, finely chopped

5 cloves garlic, peeled and minced

2 tablespoons salt

1 tablespoon coarsely ground black pepper

2 teaspoons ground juniper berries

1 piece caul fat, 10 to 24 inches long,
   or 6 strips of bacon

1 tablespoon all-purpose flour

1 tablespoon water

Preheat the oven to 350°F.

In a small saucepan over medium heat, bring the Cognac to a simmer. Light it with a match to burn off the alcohol when the flames die out. Set aside to cool.

In a large bowl, mix together the chopped meats, fatback, garlic, salt, pepper, juniper berries, and Cognac until well blended.

Line a 4 by 8-inch terrine with a lid with the caul fat (or bacon), allowing the edges to hang over the edge of the dish. Pack the meat mixture into the pan and cover with the overhanging caul. In a small bowl, mix the flour and 1 tablespoon water together to make a paste. Rub it along the edge of the dish and press the lid onto the dish. This creates a seal during the cooking process. Place the terrine in a larger ovenproof dish and pour hot water into the larger dish until it reaches halfway up the sides of the terrine.

The pâté is done when the juices run clear as it is pierced through with a knife, about 1½ hours. Remove the terrine from the oven and water bath. Remove the lid and replace it with aluminum foil. Place a heavy brick, weight, or even rocks on top to press the pâté firmly into the dish. Let the pâté cool to room temperature.

Pour off any collected juices and refrigerate the pâté for 12 to 24 hours, leaving the weight on top. Remove the weight and slice the pâté right away if you wish, or cover the terrine with plastic wrap and store for up to 10 days in the refrigerator. Cut into ½-inch-thick slices along with toasted slices of baguette, fresh radishes, and cornichon pickles.

serves 8 to 12

PISSALADIÈRE
Onion Tart

Sweet, savory, and rich pissaladière seems to me like French onion soup on bread! Never one to turn away from food, no dislikes, as I am anything but a picky eater, this traditional savory tart made with a pizza-style yeast crust, onions, olives, and fresh herbs was always and still is a favorite of mine. My brother would scrape off all the onions, push them aside on the paper, but not a problem, as I would swoop in and take his discards if I could get to the pile before my mom.

—Ethel

CRUST

2 ounces (2 scant tablespoons)
    active dry yeast

1 cup warm water (105°F)

1 teaspoon sugar

1 teaspoon salt

3½ cups all-purpose flour

Olive oil

TOPPING

8 tablespoons extra-virgin olive oil

4 tablespoons unsalted butter

15 pounds yellow onions, peeled and thinly
    sliced (7 cups)

4 fresh or 2 dried bay leaves

1 tablespoon sugar

1 teaspoon salt

2 tablespoons dry white wine

¼ cup yello cornmeal

¼ cup fresh oregano leaves, chopped

¼ cup freshly grated Parmesan cheese

12 salt-cured black olives

In a small bowl, dissolve the yeast in the warm water, add the sugar, and let stand until foamy, about 5 minutes. In a food processor fitted with a metal blade, combine the yeast mixture, salt, and 1¾ cups of the flour. Process for several minutes and add the remaining 1¾ cups of flour. Process until a dough ball forms, about 2 minutes. Turn the dough out onto a lightly floured surface and knead until the dough is elastic, 8 to 10 minutes.

Gather the dough into a ball and place in a bowl lightly coated with olive oil. Turn the dough to coat the surface with the olive oil. Cover with a clean dish towel and let rise in a warm dry place for 1 hour.

While the dough is rising prepare the topping. In a large saucepan, combine 6 tablespoons of the olive oil and the butter and melt over medium heat. When the butter begins to foam, add half of the onions, 2 fresh bay leaves, half of the sugar, and half of the salt. Stir to coat and add the remaining half of the onions, bay leaves, sugar, and salt. Cover the onions, reduce the heat to low, and cook for 20 minutes. Stir the onions and increase the heat to medium. Cook another 15 to 20 minutes, stirring occasionally. Increase the heat to high and cook, stirring constantly, until the onions caramelize to a deep golden brown, about 10 minutes. Deglaze the onions with the wine and scrape any browned bits from the sides and bottom of the pan. Cook for another 5 to 10 minutes, remove from the heat, and set aside.

Preheat the oven to 500°F.

On a lightly floured board, roll the dough out to a 30 by 20-inch rectangle. Sprinkle the cornmeal onto a baking sheet and transfer the dough. Gently press the dough to the edges of the pan, pressing upward to create an edge. Rub the remaining 2 tablespoons of olive oil over the surface. Remove the bay leaves from the onions and spread the onions over the surface of the dough. Evenly sprinkle the chopped oregano, cheese, and olives over the top. Bake until the crust is golden brown, 10 to 12 minutes, cut into squares, and serve hot or at room temperature.

serves 10 to 12

Pizza aux Anchois et Olives Noires
Pizza with Anchovies and Black Olives

No child will ever turn down pizza. They may turn their heads away at the sight of something other than your traditional pepperoni, cheese, and tomato sauce but will most likely change their minds, picking away at what they want and making a pile of what they don't want, eventually loving everything. The sight of long, hairy (I eventually accepted that they weren't hairs but tiny bones) small fish made me angry with the French people we were staying with—why on earth would they think we would enjoy this? Why are they forcing us to eat these things? One quick bite into a warm, thick crust with a soft thin layer of sauce mixed with the salty delicious kick of the anchovy changed my mind. Each town we visited on our way down south always had a boulangerie that carried them, most likely sitting in the window to beckon us one step closer to the salty pizza goodness we rarely found in the States. It was a treat we could eat on the go, in the car, wrapped up as a snack for later, or, when I was feeling adventurous, for breakfast.

—Sara

Tomato Sauce

2 pounds ripe tomatoes

2 cloves garlic

3 sprigs fresh oregano

2 fresh or 1 dried bay leaves

1 teaspoon coarse sea salt

3 tablespoons extra-virgin olive oil

Toppings

2 tablespoons extra-virgin olive oil

1 (2-ounce) jar or tin olive oil–packed anchovies

½ cup salt-cured black olives, pits removed

1 recipe crust for Pissaladière (page 25)

¼ cup yellow cornmeal

Bring a large pot of water to a boil. Using a sharp paring knife, score an X on the bottom of each tomato about ⅛ inch thick.

Using a slotted spoon, slip the tomatoes into the boiling water, working in batches if needed. Cook for 1 minute and remove from the water. Let rest until cool enough to handle. Using a sharp paring knife, cut the cores from the tomatoes and discard. Place the tomatoes into a large bowl and crush them using your hands or a wooden spoon to separate the pulp from the seeds. Transfer to a large saucepan and add the garlic, oregano, bay leaves, salt, and olive oil. Cook over low heat, uncovered, until thick, about 1 hour. For a smoother sauce, pass through a food mill and discard the solids.

Preheat the oven to 500°F.

On a lightly floured board, roll the dough out to a 30 by 20-inch rectangle. Sprinkle the cornmeal onto a baking sheet and transfer the dough. Gently press the dough to the edges of the pan, pressing upward to create an edge. For the topping, rub the 2 tablespoons of olive oil over the surface and then spread an even layer of tomato sauce over the dough. Freeze any leftover sauce for another use (it will keep for up to 1 year). Evenly scatter the anchovies and olives over the sauce. Bake until the crust barely turns golden on the edges, 7 to 10 minutes; this is not a crisp pizza. Remove from the oven, cut into squares, and serve hot or at room temperature.

serves 8 to 10

POULET RÔTI AVEC POMMES DE TERRE
Rotisserie Chicken with Potatoes

My favorite thing to do with roast chicken was tear off the crust of the freshest baguette we could find, dip it in the *poulet* drippings and bite down, slowly releasing the chicken juices from the bread. There was one time, around age ten, I remember thinking, "This is THE best thing I have ever tasted." When someone asks about the most memorable meal I've had, one of the top three is chicken, fresh off of the rotisserie. The *frites* were equally amazing; I've never found any fries in the States that compare. This was the life—crisp chicken skin, crisp duck fat fries, soft baguette soaked with the excess drippings and bits of both. A good *poulet* embodies my complete French experience: the smell of walking by those rotisserie chickens in the shop windows on a busy city street, and even better, outdoors at the market was amazing. I imagined a large smoky hand taking over my nostrils, teasing me to come closer. The sound of the chickens sizzling and the noises of the juices hitting the foil-lined rotisserie are a perfect memory from my childhood.

—Sara

1 (3- to 4-pound) roasting hen, giblets removed

1 pound small, new red, yellow, or white potatoes, peeled (peeling optional)

2 tablespoons coarse sea salt

2 tablespoons extra-virgin olive oil

½ teaspoon freshly ground black pepper

1 lemon, cut into ½-inch-thick slices

8 inches kitchen twine

Preheat the oven to 350°F.

Rinse the chicken and pat it dry. Place the potatoes in the bottom of a large roasting pan in a single layer, sprinkle 1 teaspoon of the salt over the potatoes, and drizzle with 1 tablespoon of the olive oil. Rub the chicken all over with the remaining tablespoon of olive oil, the remaining salt, and the pepper.

Tuck the slices of lemon into the chicken, and using the string, securely tie together the legs at the end joints. If using a rack, place it over the potatoes, then place the chicken, breast side up, on the rack. If not using a rack, arrange the potatoes on the edges of the pan and place the chicken directly in the pan, breast side up.

Roast the chicken in the oven until the juices run clear when a knife is inserted into the thigh, 1 to 1½ hours.

serves 4 to 6

Steak au Poivre à la Sauce aux Morilles
Pepper Steak with Morels

Steak au poivre, *steak frites*, and *entrecôtes aux echalotes* are all versions of steak with sauce and all are staples of the truckers' menu, *Le Menu Routier*. Usually there is a first course of charcuterie, a main dish of steak and sauce with *frites*, 25cl of red wine, then cheese, followed by a classic dessert such as apricot or apple tart, rice pudding, or crème caramel. And, of course, thick, dark espresso before hitting the road again, giving a boost before five or six more hours of diesel fumes and speeding cargo trucks. Here we were, the earliest days of summer sitting next to a dozen or more grizzled truckers, all having *steak au poivre*. —Ethel

4 (1-inch-thick) strip steaks, about 4 ounces each

1 tablespoon mixed green, white, and black peppercorns

1 teaspoon coarse sea salt

3 tablespoons unsalted butter

1 tablespoon extra-virgin olive oil

2 tablespoons finely chopped shallot

⅓ pound fresh morel mushrooms, cleaned and cut into halves

½ cup dry white wine

1 tablespoon coarsely chopped fresh Italian parsley

Line a baking sheet with parchment paper and lay out the steaks. In a spice grinder or mortar and pestle, crack and lightly crush the peppercorns. Rub the steaks on all sides with the salt and press the cracked peppercorns onto all sides of the meat.

Warm a large skillet over medium heat, add 2 tablespoons of the butter and the olive oil, and using a wooden spoon, stir the butter and oil together. When the butter foams, add the steaks and cook for 5 minutes. Turn the steaks, add the shallot, and continue to cook for another 5 minutes for rare, 3 to 5 minutes longer for medium. Transfer the steaks to a plate and let rest. Keep the skillet on the heat and add the mushrooms, stirring until they start to brown. Pour in the white wine and scrape the browned bits from the bottom and sides. Cook for about 1 minute longer, stir in the remaining 1 tablespoon of butter, and remove from the heat.

Place each steak on a plate and spoon the mushroom sauce evenly over the top. Sprinkle with the parsley and serve immediately.

serves 4

SANDWICHES JAMBON CRUDITÉS
Ham and Crudités Sandwiches

I always thought buying milk in France was strange; it was often in boxes on the supermarket shelf. Equally strange, there was butter on the ham sandwiches. When I first discovered this, I was disappointed as I opened my sandwich to find a big pat of butter, but changed my mind when I submitted and bit into the crusty baguette, the sweet, soft spread oozing out of the sides. The real memory of this simple recipe is in the bread—visions of driving through the French countryside swirl in my mind when I munch on a real, true French loaf—so close to perfection. Coupled with my other favorite childhood dish—poulet frites—a gorgeous baguette makes the meal. The indication of a successful road trip is the amount of crumbs on the car seat after you reach your destination.

—Sara

2 fresh, sweet baguettes
2 tablespoons salted or unsalted butter
⅓ pound white ham or other mild ham
8 slices Gruyère or Emmental cheese
12 cornichon pickles, cut in half lengthwise
⅓ pound prosciutto, thinly sliced

2 ripe tomatoes, cores removed and sliced
    crosswise into ½-inch slices
Dijon mustard
8 (10-inch) squares parchment paper
Deli tape or kitchen string

Cut the baguettes evenly into quarters crosswise, creating 8 pieces. Slice each section lengthwise and press open. Choose condiment combinations such as butter, white ham, cheese, and cornichon or prosciutto, tomatoes, and mustard.

Butter the bread on both inside pieces; layer 2 to 3 slices of ham, cheese, sliced pickles, prosciutto, tomatoes, and mustard; close the sandwich; and wrap in a sheet of parchment paper, laying the sandwich on a diagonal in the center of the paper. Fold the corner ends down over the sandwich ends and then fold the other two corners up over the sandwich middle. Secure with a small piece of tape or string. Continue with the remaining sandwiches.

serves 8

QUICHE LORRAINE

The color, the smell, and the shape—everything about Quiche Lorraine reminds me of a light, happy lunch. We often timed our long drives (sometimes upward of ten to twelve hours) to arrive at friends' houses around lunchtime. The big surprise treat was the amount of ham in my slice of quiche, and with each bite I felt as if I had won the *jambon* jackpot. (Even more so when the previous lunch plate would most likely be the traditional melon with prosciutto— sweet and salty that always left me feeling refreshed and never heavy.) The key to success of this egg tart is in the crust: you must keep it flaky and light. It always baffled me that the French had these dishes with huge amounts of cream and cheese and still managed to stay thin. My thought, as a child, was that they never actually ate like this on a daily basis; they just put their heart and soul into the prep for guests so we could pass on these amazing memories when we returned home.

—Sara

CRUST

2 cups all-purpose flour

1 teaspoon salt

8 tablespoons chilled, unsalted butter, cut into 1-inch pieces

6 tablespoons ice water

FILLING

6 eggs

2 cups half-and-half

¼ teaspoon sea salt

¼ teaspoon freshly ground black pepper

2-inch-thick slice pancetta, approximately ½ pound or ½ pound thick-cut bacon, cut into ¼-inch pieces

1 cup grated Emmental or Gruyère cheese

Preheat the oven to 350°F.

In a food processor mix together the flour and salt, then add in the butter, pulsing until the mixture resembles coarse sand. Add the chilled water a tablespoon at a time, lightly pulsing until it sticks together. Remove the dough from the food processor and form into a ball. Flatten into a 1-inch-thick disk, wrap in plastic, and chill for at least 1 hour and up to 12 hours.

To prepare the filling, combine the eggs, half-and-half, salt, and pepper in a medium bowl and whisk together and set aside.

Warm a skillet over medium heat and cook the pancetta or bacon until it begins to crisp, about 5 minutes. Using a slotted spoon, remove the pancetta or bacon and transfer to a paper towel to drain.

Remove the dough from the refrigerator and roll out on a floured surface into a 12-inch round ¼ inch thick. Gently press the crust into the dish. Allow the dough to overhang the edge of the dish by about ¼ inch and trim any excess. Pinch the edges of the dough up from the bottom, creating an edge.

Sprinkle the cheese over the bottom of the crust, then sprinkle the pancetta or bacon and finally pour the egg mixture over the top. Place on a baking sheet and transfer to the oven. Bake until it is firm to the touch and the crust just starts to turn golden, 40 to 45 minutes. When a toothpick inserted into the center comes out clean, the quiche is cooked through.

serves 6 to 8

TARTE AUX POMMES
Apple and Custard Tart

I have always remembered food in visuals, and this especially rings true with the Tarte aux Pommes. As a child, the waves of the apples in my mini dessert reminded me of the sea. I closed my eyes and bit into the soft sweetness and thoughts of the Mediterranean bounced through my head. The way the apples flowed on the pastry—I liked to pretend I was so tiny and lost in the swells of the sugary apples that I was forced to eat my way out.   —Sara

1 (10 by 15-inch) sheet puff pastry
2 Granny Smith apples, peeled, cored, and
    thinly sliced, about ¼ inch thick
1 tablespoon freshly squeezed lemon juice
¼ cup sugar

2 tablespoons cornstarch
1 tablespoon flour
1 teaspoon pure vanilla extract

Parchment paper to line the baking sheet

CUSTARD CREAM
2 cups half-and-half
3 egg yolks
½ cup sugar

GLAZE
½ cup apricot jam
2 tablespoons water

Preheat the oven to 400°F.

Remove a sheet of puff pastry from the freezer and let thaw while preparing the apples and pastry cream.

In a large bowl, toss together the apple slices, lemon juice, and sugar and set aside.

In a saucepan, warm the half-and-half over medium heat just until bubbles start to form around the edges, scalding it but not bringing it to a full boil. Remove from the heat.

In a mixing bowl, combine the egg yolks, sugar, cornstarch, flour, and vanilla and whisk together well, then slowly whisk in ½ cup of the hot half-and-half. Pour the egg mixture into the remaining hot half-and-half and return to the heat, whisking constantly for 1 to 2 minutes. Reduce the heat to low and continue whisking gently until the cream thickens and coats the back of a spoon, about 10 minutes. Immediately transfer to a clean dry bowl and press a piece of plastic wrap on the top of the custard to prevent a film from forming.

Line the baking sheet with the parchment paper and lay out the puff pastry, folding the edges up ½ inch all around and pinching to create an edge. Refrigerate until ready to use.

To make the glaze, combine the apricot jam and water in a small saucepan and cook over low heat until blended, about 2 minutes. Be careful not to overcook as it will begin to caramelize and won't spread easily over the pastry. Pass through a fine-mesh sieve.

To assemble the tart, remove the pastry sheet from the refrigerator. Spread a ¼-inch-thick layer of custard over the pastry. If you have extra custard, save for another use; it will keep for 2 to 3 days refrigerated. Arrange the apple slices, working in rows, just so they overlap. Lightly brush the tops of the apples and the crust edges with a quarter of the glaze and bake for 25 to 30 minutes, until the custard is firm and slightly golden. Remove the tart from the oven and brush the tops of the apples with the remaining glaze. Serve warm, at room temperature, or chilled.

serves 8

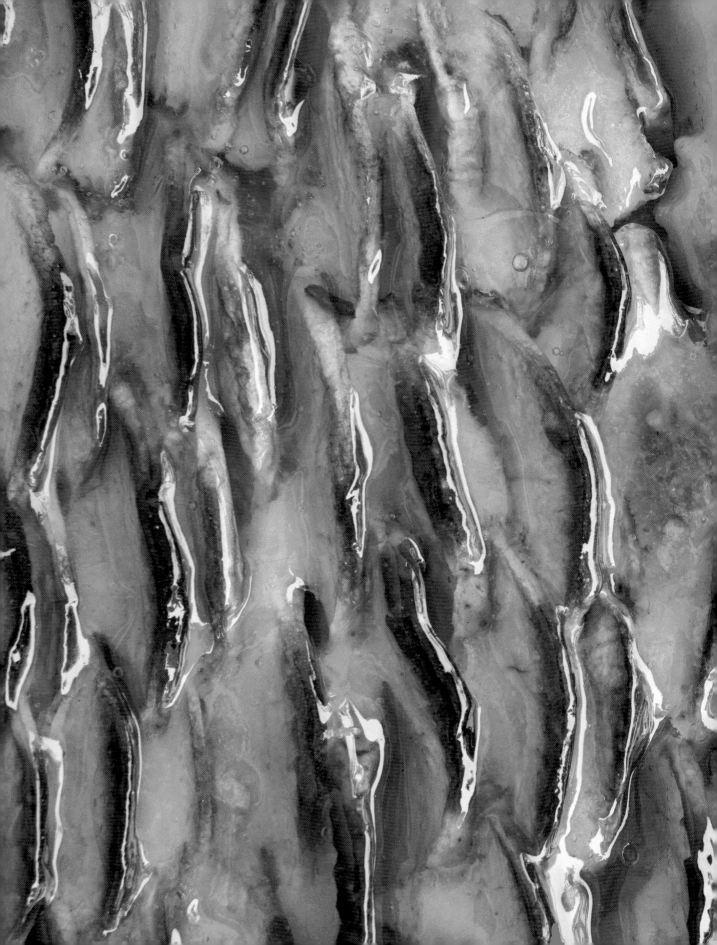

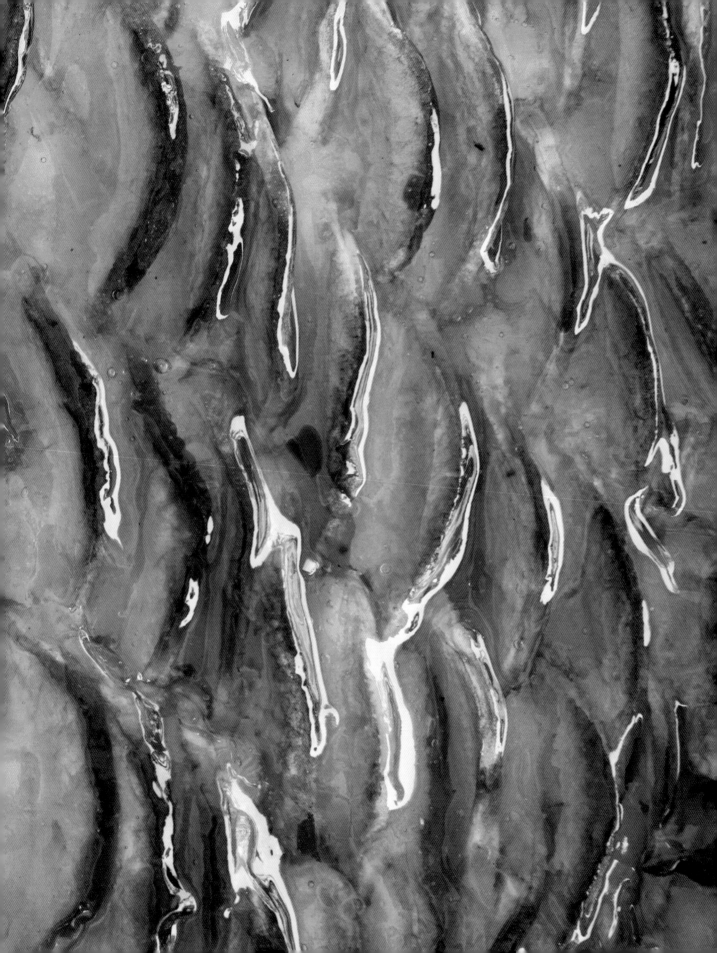

TARTE TROPÉZIENNE
Brioche Tart with Crème Pâtisserie

One summer, we were well into Provence, driving along the coast, before turning inland to our village, and the Renault broke down. There were no cell phones then, or roadside service, or even a phone number for the rental company, but a cheerful, chubby electrician on his way home for lunch got us up and running to the nearest auto shop. It was a terrible time to break down, as everything was closed for lunch and not likely to open again until early afternoon. Luckily, this day was a picnic day and we were stocked with early morning bakery purchases. We popped open the trunk of the car, laid out lunch, and sat under a roadside tree. For dessert I had chosen a wedge of *Tropézienne*, a mouthwatering brioche cake filled with soft, billowy *crème pâtisserie* and topped with crystallized sugar. The slice was easily enough for two people, but it was all mine.

—Ethel

BRIOCHE

1½ teaspoons active dry yeast

3 tablespoons warm milk

2 cups all-purpose flour

¼ teaspoon salt

2 tablespoons plus ¼ cup sugar

3 eggs

10 tablespoons unsalted butter, softened
    and cut into ½-inch pieces

Parchment paper for lining the pan

1 egg and ½ teaspoon water for the egg wash

Custard Cream from Tarte aux Pommes
    (page 34)

1 tablespoon orange blossom water

1 tablespoon kirsch along

To make the brioche, combine the yeast and warm milk in a small bowl. Let stand for a few minutes, until bubbly foam begins to form on the top. Gently stir the mixture until the yeast is dissolved.

Sift together the flour, salt, and 2 tablespoons sugar in the bowl of a stand mixer fitted with a dough hook. Add the eggs and beat for 1 minute at low speed, scraping down the sides of the bowl as needed. Add the dissolved yeast and continue beating at low speed for 5 minutes. Stop the machine, scrape the dough off the hook, and beat for another 5 minutes.

Add the butter, a few pieces at a time, beating for about 1 minute after each addition. Once all the butter has been added, beat for 10 minutes more. The dough will be very sticky and cling to your hands and the mixer. This stage of mixing is to work the butter evenly throughout the dough.

Scoop and scrape the sticky dough from the mixer, place in a large bowl, and cover with plastic wrap. Set aside in a warm place until doubled in size, 2 to 3 hours.

Gently punch down the dough, cover the bowl tightly with plastic wrap, and refrigerate overnight. The brioche will continue to rise and can easily be handled once chilled.

Once the dough is ready, place on a baking sheet pan lined with parchment paper. Pat it gently into a 12-inch circle about ¼ inch thick. Let the dough rise, uncovered, in a warm place for about 1 hour.

Preheat the oven to 400°F. Gently brush the top of the brioche with the egg wash and sprinkle with the remaining ¼ cup sugar. Bake the brioche in the center of the oven for 12 to 15 minutes. Start checking at 12 minutes; the brioche should be puffy and a light golden brown. Remove the brioche from the oven and transfer to a wire rack to cool.

Prepare the custard cream from page 34. Add the orange blossom water in kirsch along with the vanilla. Chill the custard.

To assemble, cut the brioche in half horizontally, creating two rounds, and fold them open like a sandwich. Spread all the custard cream onto the bottom layer, and gently set the top layer on the cream. Serve at room temperature.

serves 6 to 8

Chapter 2
LES MARCHÉS

TOMATES PROVENÇALES
Oven-Baked Tomatoes

PISTOU À LA PROVENÇALE
Summer Vegetable Soup

PETITES FRITURES AVEC AÏOLI
Fried Smelt with Aïoli

SALADE DE CHÈVRE CHAUD
Warm Goat Cheese Salad

LES SOLDATS
Soft-Boiled Eggs and Fresh
Asparagus Spears

CHOUX FARCIS
Stuffed Cabbage Leaves Braised
with Tomatoes

RATATOUILLE
Summer Vegetable Stew

BEIGNETS DE FLEURS DE COURGETTES
Zucchini Blossom Fritters

FRAISES AU VIN ROUGE
Strawberries in Red Wine Syrup

GÂTEAU AU FROMAGE DE CHÈVRE ET CITRON
Lemon Cheesecake

TARTE AUX FIGUES
Fresh Fig Tart

FRUITS CONFITS
Whole Candied Fruit

NOUGATINE AUX AMANDES ET MIEL
Nougatine with Almonds
and Honey

French *marchés* are defined by seasonality, and while grocery stores may stock produce from around the world at any given time of year, the markets reflect the time-honored French traditions of *terroir*—the progression of seasonal, regional produce as it is cultivated by small, land-connected farmers. No matter how fleeting the season for any given culinary treasures, they are offered up in French markets: delicate squash blossoms, two-day-old fresh goat cheeses wrapped in paper, fresh shelling beans of all colors and varieties, fruit picked that morning and meant to be eaten by dinnertime. Fresh fish, locally caught, specialty cuts of meat, and charcuterie are all displayed behind the glass of traveling vans.

Joanne and Guild, longtime family friends and fellow Americans, also moved to Provence in the 1970s, then eventually settled in Paris, but kept their Provence farmhouse. One summer I didn't return to the States with my parents, but stayed on in Provence with other family friends, Adèle and Pascal, for a memorable several months of homeschooling. I was twelve or thirteen, the perfect age to not have to go to school. Joanne and Guild, who lived nearby and were on hiatus from Paris, had taken on the task of growing corn, American super sweet varieties with hopes of selling it in the farmers' markets. In France, *maïs*, or corn, is considered animal feed, edible for people only if it comes from a can. That summer and into the fall I tagged along with Joanne and Guild to farmers' markets all over the Var, the department of the Provence where we lived. We sold corn out of a vintage baby carriage, with, in precise French script, *MAMA MAÏS* painted on the side. Our look was certainly out of place among the French farmers' tented stalls laden with tomatoes, melons, peaches, lettuce, cheese, and salamis. We looked like a ragtag trio of carnival workers. The carriage was rickety, with a black cover and huge metal wheels, and Guild always wore wire-rimmed glasses and a waistcoat-vest with a flowing shirt underneath, and Joanne a huge black sun hat and a vintage undergarment skirt. We even had a small charcoal grill set up so we could lure people with slices of sweet grilled, buttered corn. We were sure this was going to be a hit because who doesn't love corn? Well, frankly, the French don't. The following summer, we were all together again and eating corn, but the baby carriage was now available as a shopping cart or plaything, and Provence had not become the new mecca for sweet corn.

—Ethel

"Sara, hold my hand…" The comfort of my parents' voices is what I remember about the farmers' markets. Completely packed with little old ladies, children, and chefs, if I separated my hand for even a moment from my mom or dad, I felt I would be forever lost in a sea of pig heads and pantyhose. Everything was in view from an adult waist down, so what I experienced was the scene from 2½ to 3 feet high: other little kids staring at me wide-eyed as we passed each other in the stalls, butchers yelling prices as whole baby pigs stared back at me from their cases, and the sag of old women's pantyhose at their ankles, women with wheeled wire baskets in hand. The old ladies always seemed rushed and in a foul mood until you did something cute or complimented them; then they would mumble a semicoherent French sentence: "… *mon petit chouchou, oh la la, elle est gentille, elle est très très mignonne…!*" followed by plenty of unwelcomed cheek pinching.

I always found it fascinating that there was such a hubbub surrounding the freshest vegetables, meat, cheese, and fruit direct from the farmers and producers. We never did anything like that at home when I was little; it was always right there for you, neatly packaged on the shelf with a price tag. Seasonality was foreign, and often at home in upstate New York I was eating a tomato in December, wondering why it tasted like cardboard.

Provence has the most wonderful farmers' markets, a thriving tradition full of color, life, and the slower pace of a small town. It's not only a necessity to make a trip to the markets in the bigger cities near the tiny towns but also a social thing—you get to know your favorite vendors and develop a mutual love and respect. Not only are there farmers to hand you the freshest of the fresh tasty delights, there were butchers with meat that still had the animal's head attached, bakers with bread still warm to the touch, beekeepers with the thickest honey you could sculpt, cheese makers with the stinkiest rounds to make you cringe with delight.

—Sara

TOMATES PROVENÇALES
Oven-Baked Tomatoes

This simple comfort dish reminds me of the dark brown metal stove and pale yellow walls in our house in the 1980s in upstate New York. I hear and smell the juices bubbling and sizzling around the wrinkly tomatoes, taking over the entire house. I see my cute mom pulling the tomatoes out of the oven, probably wearing something similar to a form-fitting white turtle-neck with high-waisted pants (but in an adorable, fashionable way), circa 1984. The dish was easily prepared, always enjoyed by my family in the late summer/early fall when we returned from our big French summer road trip. I loved the mix of textures—salty, crunchy toasted bread crumbs with warm, soft, juicy tomato. I forced myself to not eat all of the bread crumbs first so that I would have some left over to pair with the tomato juice.   —Sara

10 to 12 medium red tomatoes

1 tablespoon finely chopped fresh rosemary

1 tablespoon finely chopped fresh thyme

2 cloves garlic, peeled and finely chopped

½ cup fine dried bread crumbs

½ teaspoon coarse sea salt

¼ cup extra-virgin olive oil

Preheat the oven to 400°F.

Cut the stems and cores from the tops of the tomatoes and place them, stem ends up, in a shallow baking dish.

In a small bowl, mix together the rosemary, thyme, and garlic, and sprinkle evenly over the tops of the tomatoes; repeat with the bread crumbs and salt. Drizzle the olive oil over the tops, letting some fall into the pan.

Roast for 20 to 25 minutes, until the tops are golden and the tomatoes have started to soften. Serve hot, warm, or at room temperature as a side dish.

serves 5 to 6

PISTOU À LA PROVENÇALE
Summer Vegetable Soup

In the small village, a crossroads really, where our childhood home in Provence sits, every neighbor has a garden. Since we were only there during the summer, we didn't have our own garden, but gracious and generous neighbors on all sides shared freely with us. One neighbor, my best girlfriend Aileen's mother, Marie Palazzoli, emigrated from Calabria in Italy to France after World War II. She and her husband, Marcel, were our closest neighbors. My brother was born while we were living in France so I spent the night with them while my parents were at the hospital. When we were older, mom would send my brother and me down the tractor road to Marie's garden, and we would pick a basket of summer vegetables, all to be tossed into a summer soup. The fun was in the picking, looking for the biggest tomatoes, tiny squash with blossoms still attached, clusters of cranberry beans with leathery pods. Once the basket was full and heavy, we lugged it up to the terrace and began shelling, peeling, and cutting. Pistou is actually a French version of pesto, which is stirred into the vegetable soup at serving time.

—Ethel

½ pound green beans

1 pound cranberry beans or other fresh shelling beans

2 tablespoons extra-virgin olive oil

2 cloves garlic, coarsely chopped

½ yellow onion, finely chopped

2 medium tomatoes, cores removed and diced

2 teaspoons coarse sea salt

1 teaspoon mixed dried herbs (rosemary, sage, thyme)

2 fresh or dried bay leaves

½ pound mixed summer squash, such as pattypan, ronde de Nice, and zucchini, cut into ½-inch cubes

½ cup vermicelli noodles

PISTOU

1 cup fresh basil leaves

3 cloves garlic, peeled

½ teaspoon sea salt

¼ teaspoon freshly ground black pepper

½ cup extra-virgin olive oil

1 tablespoon freshly squeezed lemon juice

½ cup freshly grated Gruyère cheese

Using a small knife, trim the ends from the green beans. Cut the beans into 1-inch pieces. There should be about 2 cups of chopped beans. Place in a large bowl and set aside.

Shell the cranberry beans into another bowl and set aside.

In a large soup pot, warm the olive oil over medium heat, add the garlic, and sauté until fragrant, about 1 minute. Add the onion and continue to sauté until translucent, about 5 minutes. Add the tomatoes and continue to cook until the tomatoes are soft and start to break down, about 5 minutes. Add 6 cups of water, the salt, dried herbs, and bay leaves. Increase the heat to high and bring to a boil. Boil the soup for 20 minutes, add the cranberry beans and the summer squash and cook for another 10 minutes. Add the green beans and vermicelli noodles and cook until the noodles are soft, another 5 to 10 minutes.

While the soup is cooking, prepare the pistou. In a food processor, combine the basil, garlic, salt, pepper, olive oil, and lemon juice and process until smooth, about 3 minutes. Transfer to a small bowl.

To serve, ladle the soup into bowls and drizzle the tops with 1 tablespoon of the pistou and a sprinkling of Gruyère cheese.

serves 8

PETITES FRITURES AVEC AÏOLI
Fried Smelt with Aïoli

I remember that the fishmongers, dressed in blue work coats with black rubber aprons and big boots, had their stands piled high with ice-filled wooden crates full of fish I'd never seen. There were two-foot-long eels coiled next to whiskered monkfish, clams the size of your thumbnail, strange sea snails, and sometimes even spiny sea urchins. My favorite, though, were tiny, fresh little fish, just a scant inch long, their translucent bodies only ¼ to ½ inch thick. My mom would buy several handfuls, one per person, and then we would rush home and prepare them for lunch. When they were dredged in flour, seasoned with salt and pepper, and then fried to crisp perfection, I would eat them like French fries. We still buy them now. My boys, although willing to try most things, opt for dissecting the fish, eating only the bodies, leaving small piles of heads and tails on the side.   —Ethel

AÏOLI

1 egg yolk

1 clove garlic, peeled and crushed

¼ cup coarse sea salt

¾ cup extra-virgin olive oil

FRITURES

½ pound fresh or frozen smelt, preferably
    2 inches or smaller in size

½ cup all-purpose flour

1 cup canola oil

1 teaspoon coarse sea salt

1 lemon, cut into wedges

To make the aïoli, whisk together the egg yolk, garlic, and salt until pale yellow and creamy. Whisking constantly, drizzle in the olive oil very slowly, a little at a time, until it begins to thicken. Continue until all the olive oil is incorporated.

Rinse the fish and pat dry. Place the flour on a plate and dredge the fish to coat, then place on a sheet of parchment. Prepare a large platter lined with paper towels and set aside.

Heat the canola oil in a large skillet and, using a slotted spoon, gently lower the fish into the hot oil, cooking in batches so as not to release too much moisture into the oil, which will affect the crisping. Cook the fish until they are crisp, 3 to 4 minutes. If they are small enough there is no need to turn them. Transfer the cooked fish to the paper towel–lined platter and continue until finished. Serve on a platter, sprinkled with the sea salt and with squeezed lemon wedges and a bowl of aïoli.

serves 4

SALADE DE CHÈVRE CHAUD
Warm Goat Cheese Salad

For years, until the mid-1980s when I moved to Berkeley for college, I only ever ate goat cheese in France because in California it was nowhere to be found. Every summer we would arrive in Provence and head to the nearest marché. I bee-lined for the goat cheese stand, where I chose the freshest one- or two-day-old cheeses, soft, creamy, and mild. They came beautifully wrapped in paper packets, the ends folded over like a present. Along with the freshest cheese we would also get aged goat cheeses wrapped in chestnut or grape leaves, plus other cheeses pyramid-shaped and dusted with ash. The goat cheese I love the most is aged, creamy in the middle, and with a soft gooey, wrinkly rind on the outside.   —Ethel

One 11- to 12-ounce log fresh goat cheese,
   cut crosswise into 4 even pieces
½ cup fine dried bread crumbs
⅓ pound thick slice of pancetta,
   cut crosswise into ¼-inch pieces
3 tablespoons extra-virgin olive oil
2 teaspoons red wine vinegar

1 teaspoon Dijon mustard
1 teaspoon finely chopped shallot
¼ teaspoon coarse sea salt
¼ teaspoon freshly ground black pepper
2 cups frisée greens, washed, dried, and torn
   into 1-inch pieces

Preheat the oven to 350°F.

Line a baking sheet with parchment paper and a plate with paper towels. Pat the rounds of goat cheese to a scant 1 inch thick. Place the bread crumbs on a plate, then roll each cheese round in the crumbs to coat it on all sides and place on the baking sheet several inches apart.

Place the cheese in the oven and bake until golden and soft, 8 to 10 minutes. While the cheese is baking, heat a skillet over medium heat, add the pancetta pieces, and cook, turning several times, until crisp and brown, 5 to 7 minutes. Remove from the heat and, using a slotted spoon, transfer to the paper towel–lined plate to drain.

In a large bowl, whisk together the olive oil, vinegar, Dijon mustard, shallot, salt, and pepper. Add the greens and pancetta and toss to coat. Place even amounts of the salad on four individual dinner plates and top with a baked goat cheese round. Serve warm.

serves 4

LES SOLDATS
Soft-Boiled Eggs and Fresh Asparagus Spears

How special our eggs looked in their own little porcelain containers—even more special if we were so lucky to have the little eggcups with porcelain feet. It was as if we were royalty, and our eggs were a sophisticated feast for the fanciest children around. The asparagus were our soldiers, ready to protect the drippy, bright yellow egg yolk from The Opposition (which was usually your sister or brother's finger). I loved the salt crystals—those tiny crunchy bursts of flavor that brought out the color and life of the deep green asparagus tips. I also loved pretending that the top of the egg was the crown, and when I finished gutting the shell, I daintily crowned the bottom shell and declared the hollowed egg "DONE." Eventually, I would take the top off once again, and really dig into the sides of the shell to claim the last bit of yolk with a piece of toasted brioche.

—Sara

1 pound fresh asparagus, rinsed
4 eggs

½ teaspoon coarse sea salt

To prepare the asparagus, snap the stems—they will break at the natural point of tenderness.

Fill a mixing bowl large enough to hold all the asparagus with water and ice cubes and set aside.

In a large saucepan, bring 2 cups of water to a boil over medium heat. Drop the asparagus into the boiling water and cook until fork-tender, 3 to 4 minutes. Use tongs or a slotted spoon to transfer the asparagus to the prepared ice water bath. Place an eggcup and several spears of asparagus onto individual plates.

In a saucepan over medium heat, bring 1 quart of water to a boil. Using a large spoon, gently slip the eggs into the boiling water and cook for 4 minutes. Remove the eggs and place in the eggcups. Use a small, serrated knife to cut the tops from the eggs and place next to the eggcups. Sprinkle the sea salt over the tops of the asparagus and opened eggs.

serves 4

CHOUX FARCIS
Stuffed Cabbage Leaves Braised with Tomatoes

French cabbages are different and I'm not sure I've ever seen anything like them here in the United States. The variety I'm thinking of, savoy, is huge, nearly eighteen inches in diameter, with thick, dark green leaves unfolding from the center—a real life image lifted from the still life paintings of the Dutch Masters. French cabbages, like English cabbages, are the types stories are written about, types that rabbits steal from farmers' gardens or under which people find babies. My mom is a wonderful cook, and stuffed braised cabbage is a family favorite. I was always allowed to help cook, from using a small sharp knife to cut the tough spine from the leaves or squishing up the sausage filling with my hands; no work in the kitchen was off limits.

—Ethel

3 cloves garlic, crushed

2 tablespoons extra-virgin olive oil

1 large head savoy cabbage or other variety

1½ sweet Italian sausages, casings removed

1 pound ripe tomatoes, cores removed and coarsely chopped

2 fresh or dried bay leaves

1 teaspoon coarse sea salt

½ teaspoon freshly ground black pepper

Preheat the oven to 350°F.

Rub the sides and bottom of a 9 by 13-inch baking dish with a crushed garlic clove and 1 tablespoon olive oil.

Line a baking sheet with a clean dishcloth. Bring a large pot of water to a boil. Trim the stem end of the cabbage by about ½ inch and remove 8 to 10 larger leaves from the cabbage, then, using tongs, slip the leaves one at a time into the boiling water. Blanch for 30 to 40 seconds and transfer the leaves to the baking sheet, laying them out flat. It is okay to layer them.

To make the rolls, lay out a cabbage leaf, outer side down. Place ¼ cup of the sausage at the base of a leaf and roll the leaf, stem end up, over the sausage. Fold the sides of the cabbage leaves over the sausage and continue to roll away from you. Make sure the leaf is wrapped tightly around the filling. Continue to make the rolls and fit them snugly into the baking dish.

Spread the chopped tomatoes over the tops of the cabbage rolls, drizzle with the remaining 1 tablespoon olive oil, tuck the bay leaves into the dish, and sprinkle the top with the salt and pepper.

Bake until the cabbage rolls are firm to the touch, 45 minutes to 1 hour.

serves 4 to 6

RATATOUILLE
Summer Vegetable Stew

Every Frenchman near Marseille has a ratatouille recipe and all claim theirs to be the best. As a child, my family spent many lunches with friends, people we only saw once a year, maybe just every other year, and everyone served ratatouille, with mounds of grated Gruyère cheese melted into the top. At home, pots made over the weekend would carry us through until Wednesday or longer, and now my own children love to say the singsong word, *rat-ta-touille*. But as fun as it might be to say funny sounding French words, this cornerstone dish of my childhood has not yet been embraced by my five-year-olds.   —Ethel

¼ cup extra-virgin olive oil

½ yellow onion, peeled and finely chopped

3 cloves garlic, peeled and crushed

1 large eggplant, cut into 1-inch cubes

2 medium zucchini, stem ends removed and cut into 1-inch cubes

2 red bell peppers, cut into 1-inch pieces

6 large tomatoes, cored and coarsely chopped

1 teaspoon coarse sea salt

½ teaspoon freshly ground black pepper

3 sprigs fresh thyme

2 sprigs fresh rosemary

1 fresh or dried bay leaf

½ cup grated Gruyère or Emmental cheese

In a large soup pot, warm the olive oil over medium heat. Add the onion and garlic and stir until soft and fragrant, 3 to 4 minutes. Stir in the eggplant, zucchini, and peppers. Cook until the vegetables are soft and just starting to brown, about 5 minutes. Add the tomatoes, salt, and pepper and stir together. Reduce the heat to low and cover.

Prepare a bouquet garni by gathering the thyme, rosemary, and bay leaf together and tying them at the stem end with kitchen twine. Add the herbs to the pot and continue to cook, stirring often. As the juices begin to evaporate, add 1 cup water, a quarter cup at a time.

Cook for 1 hour. Serve with the cheese sprinkled over individual servings.

serves 6 to 8

BEIGNETS DE FLEURS DE COURGETTES
Zucchini Blossom Fritters

Picking zucchini blossoms is the best part of this dish, except for dipping the piping hot fritters in crunchy sea salt before gobbling them down. The deeply funneled flowers wilt so quickly that harvesting and cooking need to happen practically within minutes. But before cooking, Aileen, my Provençal neighbor and playmate, and I were given the job of picking out the pollen-covered stamens, which stained our fingers bright yellow. And then we needed to make sure no little garden bugs remained, dusting out any pincher bugs, aphids, or other little creatures that found the flowers as delectable as we did.

—Ethel

10 to 12 fresh zucchini blossoms

1 cup all-purpose flour

½ teaspoon baking powder

½ teaspoon salt

1 egg

¾ cup milk

3 cups canola or other light vegetable oil

½ teaspoon coarse sea salt, for serving

To prepare the blossoms, gently trim the stamens from the inside the flowers, rinse them if needed, and pat dry.

To make the batter, stir together the flour, baking powder, and salt in a medium bowl. Then whisk in the egg and milk until well blended with no lumps of flour.

Line a platter with paper towels and set aside.

In a large skillet over medium high heat, warm the oil until it sizzles when a teaspoon of the batter is dropped in. Working in batches of 3 to 4, dredge the blossoms in the batter and using tongs or a slotted spoon, let the excess batter drip off and gently lower them into the hot oil. Cook for 1 to 2 minutes, then turn and cook another 1 to 2 minutes, until the blossoms are a light golden brown. Transfer to the paper towel–lined platter and continue until all are cooked. Serve hot, sprinkled with the coarse sea salt.

serves 6

FRAISES AU VIN ROUGE
Strawberries in Red Wine Syrup

It is true that children in France are allowed to taste wine, and yes, champagne too. There was always a little teaspoon or two stirred into my glass of water. It was not very appealing, bitter, like sour grapes, but thrilling nonetheless. For champagne we were always offered our own flute, just a drop or two, for cheers and to get the palate ready. At home in California, any food prepared with alcohol was for the grown-ups, which was fine with me, since bourbon-laced pound cakes and brandy-filled cherries just didn't have the same appeal as the sugary wine sauce that collected at the bottom of my bowl of strawberries.   —Ethel

2 pints medium-size ripe strawberries, stems removed and cut into halves

¼ cup sugar

1 cup red wine, such as Côtes de Provence or Côtes du Rhône

Place the strawberries in a large mixing bowl. Sprinkle the sugar over the tops of the strawberries and gently toss to coat. Add the red wine and gently stir the strawberries, then place in the refrigerator for at least 30 minutes and up to 1 hour. Serve chilled.

serves 4

GÂTEAU AU FROMAGE DE CHÈVRE ET CITRON
Lemon Cheesecake

During our summer visits to Provence, we always hiked up into the Alps-Maritimes to see our friends Mark and Nina in the forest. There was no driving road, so we hiked in about an hour, or sometimes Mark would meet us at the bottom of the trail with two donkeys, one for our backpacks and one for my brother and me. Oliver would ride in front, clutching the short cropped mane. I sat on the back, balancing as best I could while the donkey swayed back and forth along the rocky, uneven hillside trail. Mark and Nina made goat cheese for a living, hiking out of the mountains several times a week to sell cheese at the local markets, and while we were visiting we ate a lot of cheese. There were fresh curds with wild berry jam for breakfast, stuffed baked vegetables, and, at least once a visit, a rich, lemon cheesecake. Because they had neither gas nor electricity, the cake was baked in a wood-fired oven, and the resulting texture was wonderfully light and crumbly.

—Ethel

CRUST

1½ cups walnut halves

¼ cup loosely packed light brown sugar

20 plain water crackers, broken into 1-inch pieces

½ teaspoon freshly grated nutmeg

6 tablespoons unsalted butter, melted

FILLING

15 ounces soft goat cheese

16 ounces mascarpone

3 tablespoons finely grated lemon zest

4 large eggs, lightly beaten

1⅓ cups granulated sugar

½ teaspoon salt

To make the crust, combine the walnuts, brown sugar, crackers, and nutmeg in a food processor fitted with the metal blade. Process until finely ground. Add the melted butter and continue to process until the mixture is moist and sticks to the sides of the processor bowl. Gather the mixture together and place in the center of a 9- or 10-inch springform pan. Using your fingertips, gently press the crumb mixture evenly over the bottom and two-thirds up the sides of the pan. Put in the freezer to chill for 15 minutes.

Preheat the oven to 350°F.

To make the filling, first rinse out the food processor bowl, then again fit it with the metal blade. Place the goat cheese, mascarpone, lemon zest, eggs, sugar, and salt in the bowl, and process until smooth and creamy. Remove the springform pan with the crust from the freezer, place in the center of a baking sheet, and pour the filling into the crust. Bake until the top springs back when lightly pressed with a fingertip, about 1 hour. Remove from the oven and let cool to room temperature or transfer to the refrigerator to cool for at least 1 hour and up to overnight. When completely cool, release the sides of the springform pan and transfer the cheesecake to a serving plate. Serve chilled or at room temperature, cut into slices.

serves 10 to 12

TARTE AUX FIGUES
Fresh Fig Tart

I love how nature can make something so perfectly beautiful and so delicious as a fig. The insides are magical—how on earth can that color happen? There was always a fig tree in the backyard of our friend's house near Aix-en-Provence, and the closer I walked to the tree, the more bee buzz I heard. The bees must have been having a party, happily feasting on the sugary drips from the ends of the ripe figs. I loved splitting the figs open and eating them from the inside out—I wasn't sure if the skins would give me a stomachache, so I just devoured the pulp. Running through a big backyard or field, I would eventually stumble upon some figs and ruin my dinner, eating no less than about ten at a time.

—Sara

CRUST

2 cups all-purpose flour

1 teaspoon salt

¼ cup sugar

8 tablespoons chilled unsalted butter, cut into 1-inch pieces

6 tablespoons ice water

1 egg

Custard Cream from Tarte aux Pommes recipe (page 34)

12 ripe figs, cut into quarters lengthwise

GLAZE

½ cup currant jelly

Preheat the oven to 400°F.

To make the crust, mix together the flour, salt, and sugar in a food processor fitted with the metal blade attachment. Then add the butter, pulsing until the mixture resembles coarse sand. Add the chilled water, a tablespoon at a time, lightly pulsing until it sticks together. Remove the dough from the food processor and form into a ball. Flatten into a 1-inch-thick disk, wrap in plastic, and chill for at least 1 hour and up to 12 hours.

Remove the dough from the refrigerator and roll out to a 12-inch round, ¼ inch thick. Gently press the dough into a tart pan with a removable bottom. Lay a sheet of parchment over the pastry and top with baking weights or dry beans (kidney, lentil, whatever is on hand). Return the tart to the refrigerator and chill for 30 minutes.

While the tart crust is chilling, prepare an egg wash by lightly beating an egg with a tablespoon of water.

Bake the tart shell for 30 minutes, until just golden. Remove from the oven, brush with the egg wash, and return to the oven for 5 minutes. Remove the crust from the pan and let it cool.

Spread the custard cream evenly over the bottom of the tart shell. Layer the fig quarters, skin side down, and fitting tightly together in concentric circles starting from the center and working outward.

To prepare the glaze, bring the currant jelly and 2 tablespoons of water to a boil and cook for 2 minutes. Remove from the heat and, using a pastry brush, gently coat the tops of the figs. Chill for 30 minutes to 1 hour.

serves 6 to 8

FRUITS CONFITS
Whole Candied Fruit

Fruitcake speckled with tiny shards of hard, fluorescent, sugared fruit and maraschino cherries summed up my California experience of candied fruit. But nothing prepared me for the Provençal counterparts of whole candied pear, entire rounds of pineapple, tiny clementines, cherries still with pits and stems, and any other fruit you could possibly imagine. The exotic displays, dripping with sugar, conjured images of eighteenth-century decadence and frivolity. The candied fruit were layered in trays and packed delicately in tiny boxes with cellophane wrapping, and decorated the windows of candy and pastry shops and market stalls in Provence. Buying them was such a treat, but they were so delicate and toylike, how could I possibly eat them? The fruit is simmered in sugar syrup for 20 minutes, then letting the fruit stand overnight in the syrup, and repeating the cooking process every 24 hours for 6 days.

—Ethel

1 pound small clementines (about 10), the peels each pricked several times with a pin

2½ cups sugar
¼ cup corn syrup

Fill a pot large enough to hold the fruit with water and bring to a boil over high heat. Blanch the fruit in the boiling water by submerging them for 1 minute. Remove the fruit from the water, using a slotted spoon, and transfer to a plate. Pour out the water and return the pot to the stove. Stir together the sugar with 5 cups of water and bring to a boil, then cook, stirring constantly, until the sugar has dissolved and stir in the corn syrup. Transfer the fruit to the pot, reduce the heat to a simmer, and cook for 20 minutes.

Remove the pot from the heat and let cool for 24 hours. The next day bring the syrup and fruit back to a boil, reduce to a simmer and cook for 20 minutes, then remove from the heat and let cool. Repeat this process of cooking for 20 minutes and letting the fruit stand in the liquid for 24 hours, 4 more times, for a total of 6 cooking sessions over a period of 6 days.

On the last day of cooking, place a wire rack in the middle of a baking sheet lined with parchment paper. Repeat the cooking process, cooking for 20 minutes. Remove the fruit from the pot and transfer to the cooling rack, stem end up. Let cool for 24 hours. To store, place in a single layer in an airtight container and keep in a cool, dry place for up to 24 months.

makes 10 candied clementines

NOUGATINE AUX AMANDES ET MIEL
Nougatine with Almonds and Honey

A spoonful of French honey is heaven. It has a subtle grit and texture that, to an American kid who's used to the corn syrup-like honey in the plastic bear bottle, may seem off, but it's perfection. It's thick and lovely and comes in all different colors. It's delicate and fresh and boasts subtle floral notes; you know that the bees were working hard in those lavender patches. I always loved bees; they are so focused and never have any hesitation to risk their lives for their lovely queen. What funny thoughts I had in my seven-year-old head: The bees were on a mission much like the buzz of rush hour in Grand Central Station, all quickly and fiercely going about their work, wearing tiny three-piece suits and carrying tiny briefcases, getting paid with tiny jars of honey!

—Sara

1 teaspoon vegetable oil, such as canola

1 (8 by 11-inch) sheet of edible wafer paper, also called rice paper or alternatively parchment paper (wafer papers available in specialty cooking shops or online)

1 cup coarsely chopped unsalted almonds

1 cup sugar

2 tablespoons honey

Preheat the oven to 250°F.

Rub the sides and bottom of an 8 by 8-inch baking dish with the vegetable oil, line with the wafer paper or parchment, and set aside.

Place the almonds in a single layer on a baking sheet and bake until fragrant, turning once, 8 to 10 minutes. Remove from the oven and transfer to a plate.

In a heavy-bottomed saucepan, place the sugar, then layer the honey and the almonds. It is important not to mix them. Warm the mixture over medium heat without stirring. Once the sugar begins to melt, using a wooden spoon or silicone spatula, mix the nuts into the sugar and honey, continuing to stir until the sugar has completely dissolved. Stop stirring and let the sugar cook until it turns a medium golden brown, 3 to 6 minutes. Watch closely as the mixture can burn very quickly.

Pour the mixture into the prepared baking dish and, working quickly, spread to coat the bottom of the pan evenly. Let cool, turn out from the dish, and break into 1-inch pieces.

makes about 2 cups

Chapter 3
STREET FOOD

BEIGNETS
French Donuts

MERGUEZ
Spicy Grilled Lamb Sausage Patties

PAN BAGNAT
Niçoise-Style Tuna Sandwich

GLACE À LA PISTACHE
Pistachio Ice Cream

MARRONS GRILLÉS
Roasted Chestnuts

PRALINES
Candied Peanuts

SOCCA
Chickpea Flour Crepes

CRÊPES SALÉES ET SUCRÉES
Sweet and Savory Crepes:
Chestnut Cream and Vanilla Ice Cream,
Banana-Honey and Almond,
Ham and Cheese

Although France is not particularly known for street food cuisine, what is available is delectable and uniquely regional, such as the buttery chickpea flour crepes historically cooked in three-foot-diameter pans on charcoal ovens in Nice, spicy grilled merguez sausage served on a baguette and doused with fragrant red harissa sauce, while sweet and savory crepes, salty sugared pralines, and powdered sugar–covered beignets, or French-style donuts, seem prevalent everywhere. Whenever we were out and about, visiting ancient castle ruins, hiking down the arid cliffs of the Mediterranean coast to get to the perfect beach, or wandering city streets, street food seemed common fare. As our families settled in for the summer, the long trek to the south behind us, the next weeks promised an itinerary of day trips to historic sites, favorite villages, and visits with friends. This life on the go was meant for street food, and we intended to try it all.

Meals are not had on the run in France, so street food is limited mostly to snacks or treats. Hot pralines are sold in markets and festivals year-round, and in winter, chestnuts. The smell of charred chestnut shells mingled with the unctuous smell of butter melted in sugar is too tempting to pass by. In Paris and Provence, spicy grilled merguez sausages are cooked in stands found throughout parks and market entrances. And ice cream, the quintessential street food, can be found everywhere in every possible flavor, uncluttered with chunks and the saccharine sweet additives found in American ice cream. As we were often on the go—tourists and unconstrained by the cultural traditions of long meals—we tried any street food we could find: chickpea crepes and *pan bagnat* in Nice, beignets at the beach and carnivals, pizzas from wood-fired ovens on trucks, and ice cream.

The Gorges du Verdon is a deep river canyon that runs through the craggy, sparse hills of Alpes-de-Haute-Provence, once known as the Basses-Alpes. The water of the Verdon River is icy cold and deep turquoise in color. In 1974, when I was six, the massive dam built to trap the river became operational. The rising water swallowed up the village of Les-Salles-Sur-Verdon, which now lies beneath the deep waters of the lake created by the dam. This underwater ghost town captivated my imagination, and I dreamed of diving down and swimming through the ancient stone buildings, in and out of windows, seeing what people might have left behind. A new, higher village was built, but its 1970s architecture is strikingly out of place in a landscape of centuries-old stone villages. The summer the dam was built we began going to the lake. In theory we were not very many kilometers away, but the reality of the single lane and switchback mountain roads made the day trip nearly two hours either way, at least to the part of the lake we loved the most, the town of Bauduen. Bauduen had a smooth pebble beach, just like Nice, a poor man's Côte d'Azur. The days were long and sun-drenched, filled with beach towels, umbrellas, books, watercolors for painting landscapes on flat river rocks, and picnics. I always loved the areas of the lake that were walking distance to a café, which allowed for double ice cream cones and other treats. At the end of the day, we might be lucky enough to catch a pizza truck with a wood-fired oven parked along the edge of the water, and pizza would be dinner. La Reine, a pizza with a cracker-thin crust, oregano-infused tomato sauce, white ham, cheese, and thinly sliced mushrooms from a can was my favorite. The pizzas were small and shared nothing in common with thick-crust American pizzas that come in super sizes. I ordered my own pizza, only needing to share if someone had something I wanted to try.

Down the mountain and across the low rolling hillsides and valley vineyards was the Mediterranean, also a day's trip from our home. Here the air was sticky and salty, and the

water buoyant and shallow for miles, or at least it seemed. We mostly had picnics, but always were allowed treats from the beach vendors. My favorite story, and I tell this with sadness as the practice is all but extinct now, is of the vendors that used to walk back and forth along the beach carrying large shallow baskets piled with cream-filled beignets. Bakery fresh, or so I believed, and wrapped in sheets of parchment, the beignets were always piping hot and dusted with sugar, and each bite forced a thick ooze of a pastry cream, custard, or cherry jelly to drip from the opposite end. They are now replaced by industrially baked versions and sold from rolling carts fitted with freezers for ice cream, so the handcrafted French donuts of my childhood are seemingly gone, at least from the beaches.

—Ethel

We were so fortunate to be able to travel throughout France for such a long time during the summer months. To make this work financially, we ate on the cheap: lots of picnics and street food instead of restaurants and cafés. When the dollar was bad, my dad would sometimes secretly swipe an espresso cup from a café, putting it in my mom's purse and justifying this by confidently stating that since the coffees cost twice as much as they did back home, it was like he was "buying" the cup from the place. This somehow made sense to me, but as I got older I realized you were not only paying for the coffee but the experience of the café—the street was your television, a Parisian reality show in real time.

Street food seemed abundant; just like the hot dog vendor is to New York City, the crepe vendor is to Paris. I distinctly remember the smells of gamey merguez sizzling on the grill on the street—it reminded me of backyard BBQ at home. I had my go-to street favorites, one of which was the *crêpe au sucre*, a beautiful thin pancake with a layer of white sugar, neatly folded into a triangle, placed in a parchment cone, steaming hot. The sugar slowly melted in the crepe in the tightly packed triangle, and I was nearly salivating uncontrollably before it even reached my hands.

Mediterranean beach days were a similar food experience—gather as many inexpensive items as possible and munch throughout the afternoon and early evening. There was always a baguette, some pâté, *jambon*, dry *saucisson*, maybe a bit of cheese wrapped up from the previous night's dinner, yogurt, granola bars, apricots, and a token candy bar (most likely a Lion bar—the equivalent of a Kit Kat and 100 Grand bar rolled into one). We never sat longer than five minutes to eat, rejecting the "wait forty minutes" rule before you jump back into the sea. Hike down to the water, run over the hot stones or hot sand (hopping the entire way, *Ow! Ow! Ow!*), jump in the water, start to get a little chilly, run back for the towel, stuff your face with a piece of baguette and ham, run back to the water, and repeat until almost dusk. I was a skinny little kid with birdlike legs, but I always had a giant appetite and could eat at least four or five sandwiches in one beach session. The best part about this whole experience was the ice cream boat—it would arrive at the edge of the shore, bells ringing, ready to sell me my favorite cone. I always chomped at the bottom of the cone first because there was a piece of chocolate at the tip. While finishing the ice cream, the vanilla would leak through the hole in the cone all over my hands, on to my feet and bathing suit. Jumping in the Mediterranean one more time would always take care of those messy drips.

—Sara

BEIGNETS
French Donuts

Beignets always reminded me of summer carnivals at home in the United States. They had that distinct funnel cake smell and were essentially the same thing—deep-fried dough covered in a layer of powdered sugar sometimes so thick you couldn't see the light brown color of the beignets. As kids, we used to blow the powdered sugar on each other; the beautiful snowy mound was there to be played with. As I bit down into each puff, I could hear the sound of the carnival—laughter and screams from the ferris wheel, dance music played loudly through bad, crackling speakers, and balloons being popped at the dart game. Every summer we got our carnival fix in Paris at the Jardin des Tuileries, always starting with *la Grande Roue* (the big ferris wheel) and continuing on to the terrifying haunted house we had to walk through. We'd finish the carnival fun by sitting on the stone steps of the entrance to the park, a box of beignets in our lap, laughing until our stomachs hurt. We talked about what happened earlier that day, which usually involved me burrowing my face in my sister's shoulder while we walked through the haunted house, so terrified I could barely move, convinced we would never get out of there alive to enjoy our box of delicious beignets. —Sara

1 cup warm whole milk (about 110°F)

½ cup granulated sugar

¼-ounce package dry yeast

1 egg, lightly beaten

4 tablespoons unsalted butter, melted

½ teaspoon salt

½ teaspoon pure vanilla extract

1 tablespoon orange flower water

4 cups all-purpose flour

4 to 6 cups canola oil

¼ cup powdered sugar

Pour the warm milk into a large bowl. Mix in 1 tablespoon granulated sugar and sprinkle the yeast over the top. Let stand until the yeast begins to bubble, about 5 minutes.

Whisk the egg, butter, salt, vanilla, the remaining sugar, and the orange flower water into the milk. Add 2 cups of flour and work into the wet ingredients using a wooden spoon. Add another cup of flour and gather the dough into a ball. It will be sticky. Knead the dough and add the remaining flour, ¼ cup at a time, until it forms a smooth yet soft ball; stop adding flour at this point. Transfer the dough to a clean bowl, cover with plastic wrap, and let rise for 1½ hours.

Transfer the dough to a floured work surface and roll out to a 1-inch-thick rectangle. Cut the dough lengthwise into 4 pieces, then cut it crosswise into 6 pieces, creating 24 small beignets. Cover the dough with a clean, dry dish towel and let rise for 1 hour.

In a large deep skillet over high heat, warm the oil until it reaches 350°F. Use a candy thermometer to check the temperature. Fry the beignets in small batches of 2 to 3 in the hot oil, turning them every 30 seconds or so with tongs, until they are puffed and golden brown all over. They cook quickly and will start to burn if left too long in the oil. Remove the beignets from the oil and drain on paper towels. Put the powdered sugar into a fine-mesh strainer and dust the warm beignets generously with the powdered sugar. Serve immediately.

makes 24 beignets, serves 8

MERGUEZ
Spicy Grilled Lamb Sausage Patties

I was amazed how little you had to do with merguez—they were so full of game and flavor that we never added a thing. We just threw them on the grill, turning every few minutes, next to a halved baguette toasting on the side. My bare feet felt so good on the cool stone tiles of the kitchen floor while I ate the hot, spicy merguez. That was what was so great about the French kitchen in the summertime—no matter how hot the weather was, you could always count on the kitchen floor being cold. I would lie flat on the ground with my head to the side, my ear pressing up against the tile, listening with the other ear to the sounds of chopping, sizzling, and copper pots clanging, watching from a small dog's-eye view what was happening below everyone's knees. I would close my eyes and daydream while my merguez and baguette would be waiting patiently for me on the kitchen table on a paper napkin.   —Sara

DRY SPICE MIX

¼ cup sweet paprika

2 tablespoons fennel seeds

2 tablespoons ground cumin

1 tablespoon coriander seeds

2 tablespoons course sea salt

½ teaspoon ground cinnamon

½ to 1 teaspoon cayenne pepper

¾ teaspoon black peppercorns

Combine all the spices in a spice grinder or mortar and pestle and grind until the mix is a well-blended powder. Transfer to an airtight container.

HARISSA

12 dried red chile peppers (about 1 ounce)

1 teaspoon coarse sea salt

½ teaspoon ground coriander seeds

¼ cup extra-virgin olive oil

½ teaspoon ground caraway seeds

4 cloves garlic, peeled

2 teaspoons lemon juice

As with the spice mix, combine all the ingredients in a spice grinder or mortar and pestle and mix until a smooth paste forms. Transfer to an airtight container and refrigerate until needed.

SAUSAGE PATTIES

2 pounds ground lamb

8 ounces ground or finely chopped lamb fat
(ask the butcher to give you trimmings)

6 cloves garlic, finely chopped

2 tablespoons chopped fresh cilantro

¼ cup dry spice mix

2 tablespoons harissa

½ cup Dijon-style mustard

2 baguettes, cut into quarters crosswise

Preheat a charcoal grill to a high heat. Line a baking sheet with parchment paper and set aside.

In a large bowl mix together by hand the lamb, lamb fat, garlic, cilantro, dry spice mix, and harissa. Mix well, kneading together the ingredients until the meat is infused with the spices. Gather about ¾ cup (about 5½ ounces) of the mixture and shape into a log 5 to 6 inches long by 1 inch wide. Place on the baking sheet and repeat until all the meat is shaped. Place the sausages on the grill and cook for 4 to 5 minutes, then turn and cook the other side, another 4 to 5 minutes. Alternatively, warm a large skillet over medium-high heat and cook for 4 to 5 minutes on both sides.

To serve, spread about 1 teaspoon of mustard on the insides of the baguettes and add a sausage.

makes 8 sandwiches

PAN BAGNAT
Niçoise-Style Tuna Sandwich

The beaches of Nice are rocky, not sharp rock, but a jumble of smooth pebbles, black, gray, speckled brown, and white. Candy shops and bakeries all over Nice sell bags of candies fashioned after these pebbles. It was important to have plastic jellies—sandals—to protect your feet. Thankfully the jellies are sold on every street corner in every color. Mine were hot pink one year and cerulean blue the next. Not great for blisters, but better a blister or two than walking on stones all day. Along with jellies and pebble beaches, Nice also has the best tuna sandwiches in the world: vegetables, vinaigrette, and tuna, all soaked into a soft white roll, the best possible beach lunch.

—Ethel

4 round sandwich rolls or 8-inch-long baguette slices

¼ cup extra-virgin olive oil

4 teaspoons red wine vinegar

2 ripe medium tomatoes, cut into 8 (¼-inch-thick) slices

4 hard-boiled eggs, peeled and sliced lengthwise into ¼-inch slices

8 olive oil–packed anchovy fillets

12 fresh basil leaves

4 radishes, cut into ⅛-inch-thick slices

12 black olives, pits removed and crushed

4 (⅛-inch-thick) slices mild red or yellow onions

4 red or green oak leaf lettuce leaves

1 (5-ounce) can tuna, packed in water, drained

1 teaspoon freshly ground black pepper

1 teaspoon coarse sea salt

To make the sandwiches, slice the rolls or baguette lengths in half, opening up to a sandwich. Baste both insides of all the pieces of bread with the olive oil, using up the ¼ cup. Sprinkle a teaspoon of vinegar evenly over the bread in each sandwich. Layer the ingredients on the bottom slice of bread, beginning with the tomato slices, eggs, anchovy fillets, basil, radish slices, olives, onions, lettuce, and tuna. Season with the pepper and salt, and top with the remaining bread slices.

serves 4

GLACE À LA PISTACHE
Pistachio Ice Cream

I can't enjoy ice cream without a cone. I need a bit of texture with the creamy and the crunch of a wafer cone, which after two scoops of ice cream is the perfect grand finale. One thing France has that I haven't seen anywhere else is the double cone, two separate cups for ice cream at the end of the cone handle, a genius idea where, when melting, both the ice creams would begin to converge into one unique flavor at the tip of the cone. This is where my habit of eating the end of the cone first came into play—I impatiently wanted to taste both the ice creams together right away, through my upside-down wafer straw. I'm not sure if I truly loved *cassis* or if I just liked saying it—the word was so beautiful, and I was proud of myself when I communicated what I wanted in French at such a young age.   —Sara

2 vanilla beans

2 cups heavy cream

1 cup whole milk

½ cup honey

1 tablespoon brandy

1 cup toasted, coarsely chopped, unsalted
    pistachios

Cut the vanilla beans in half lengthwise and scrape out the seeds. Place both the seeds and the vanilla pods in a saucepan, along with the heavy cream, milk, honey, and brandy. Warm the mixture over medium heat, stirring constantly until tiny bubbles begin to form at the edges, about 10 minutes. Remove from the heat and continue to stir, making sure the honey is completely dissolved. Remove and discard the vanilla pods.

Transfer the mixture to a large bowl or pitcher and chill for at least 2 hours and up to 24 hours. Transfer to an ice cream maker, add the toasted pistachios, and process according to the manufacturer's instructions. Cover and transfer to the freezer for an additional 2 hours to allow the ice cream to set.

serves 6 to 8

MARRONS GRILLÉS
Roasted Chestnuts

In Provence, the chestnut trees are sometimes terraced along the hillsides. When we visited our friends Mark and Nina who lived deep in the backcountry beyond Nice, we hiked through acres and acres of seemingly abandoned chestnut orchards. The wide, flat leaves created a canopy of shade for the long hike to their farmhouse, and we walked through carefully because beekeepers kept their hives there so the bees would make rich, dark, chestnut honey.

—Ethel

2 pounds chestnuts

Prepare a charcoal grill or preheat the oven to 500°F.

If using a grilling basket, place this on the grill to heat before adding the chestnuts.

To prepare the chestnuts, score the tough outer peel by cutting a ½-inch X on the flat side of the chestnut. This is essential as the chestnuts will explode if the hot air is not able to escape from the shell during cooking.

When the grill is ready, place the chestnuts in the hot grilling basket and cook, turning several times, until the peels darken and the score marks begin to crack open, about 5 minutes. In the oven, place the scored chestnuts on a baking sheet and roast in the oven, turning several times, until the score marks begin to crack open and the peels begin to darken, about 15 minutes.

serves 4 to 6

PRALINES
Candied Peanuts

On the streets of lake towns, beach boardwalks, and cobblestone market streets, vendors set up wood-fired deep skillets, similar to a wok. They rolled peanuts around and around the sides of the pan, with each turn thickening their crunchy coating of caramelized sugar and butter. As people passed by, especially kids, they thrust out samples of the crunchy peanuts encrusted in a sweet sugar coating, chanting, "*Goûtez, goûtez, pour la petite.*" If we were lucky, we'd get three; if we were really lucky we had enough change in our pockets to buy the little cellophane bags tied with red baker's string. The only way to eat them was to lightly crunch through the coating, revealing the salty nuts.

—Ethel

8 ounces raw peanuts with skins

½ cup sugar

¼ cup water

1 teaspoon pure vanilla extract

½ teaspoon coarse sea salt

Preheat the oven to 350°F.

In a large skillet over medium heat, dry roast the peanuts until they just begin to toast and lightly brown, 5 to 7 minutes. Remove the skillet from the heat and gently stir in the sugar, water, the vanilla, and salt. Return the skillet to the stovetop and continue to cook over medium heat, stirring constantly, until the sugar begins to caramelize, about 10 minutes. The liquid will thicken and coat the peanuts. When this happens, transfer the peanuts to a baking sheet and spread them out. Place the peanuts in the oven to finish cooking, about 10 minutes until caramel in color.

Once completely cooled, store the peanuts in an airtight container.

makes about 2 cups

SOCCA
Chickpea Flour Crepes

Nowadays, I think there is only one street vendor in Nice who makes socca, the thick chickpea flour crepe, that is a specialty of this port city (and was once a sailor's breakfast decades ago). Socca now is sold all over the city in restaurants, bistros, and cafés. But as far as I can tell, there is only one or two street vendors who still make and sell socca on charcoal stoves. As a child, I have vague memories of rustic charcoal stoves set up along the Promenade des Anglais, just steps from the water, with people making and selling socca, serving it up in brown paper with a pat of butter. I must confess, though, that it might only be a figment of my imagination, woven into my memories from old postcards.   —Ethel

1 cup chickpea flour

1 teaspoon sea salt

1½ teaspoons freshly ground black pepper

1 cup lukewarm water

4 to 6 tablespoons extra-virgin olive oil

Sift the chickpea flour into a bowl and whisk in the salt and pepper, then slowly pour in the water, whisking it to avoid lumps. Whisk in 2 tablespoons of the olive oil. Cover and refrigerate overnight.

To cook, heat about 1 tablespoon of olive oil in a frying pan over medium-high heat. Stir the batter well. When the oil is hot, pour a thin layer of the batter into the pan and cook until the edges brown and curl slightly, about 2 minutes. Turn and cook the other side, another 2 minutes. Repeat until the batter is gone, adding more oil to the pan as needed. Serve hot or warm with butter, tapenade, or goat cheese.

makes about 5 crepes

CRÊPES SALÉES ET SUCRÉES
Sweet and Savory Crepes

Chestnut Cream and Vanilla Ice Cream, Banana-Honey and Almond, Ham and Cheese

This is my go-to crepe. I was never really into savory crepes, and the smell and sounds of Paris always had me craving a sweet one. *Crêpe au Sucre* is just so simple and amazing. I discovered over the years that honey gives it the sweet touch I need, and it is healthier than white sugar. As my crepe was being made, I was always lifted up by my dad since I was too short to see my favorite part through the little plastic window: the crepe batter being perfectly, evenly spread by the wooden T-shaped stick. When I finished devouring the most delicious, thin pancake in the world, I was on the razor edge of sweetness overdose, but so happy.

—Sara

BASIC CREPE RECIPE

(for savory, eliminate the sugar and
increase the salt to ½ teaspoon)

½ cup all-purpose flour

½ cup whole milk

¼ cup warm water

2 large eggs

2 tablespoons unsalted butter, melted, plus
2 tablespoons for cooking

1½ teaspoons sugar

¼ teaspoon salt

The best pan to use is a small, 8-inch nonstick sauté pan. In a blender, combine the flour, milk, water, eggs, melted butter, sugar, and salt. Process until smooth, transfer the blender pitcher to the refrigerator, and chill for at least 30 minutes and up to 2 days.

To make the crepes, heat the remaining 2 tablespoons of butter in an 8-inch nonstick sauté pan over high heat. Pour about ¼ cup of batter into the center of the pan. Lift the pan from the burner and swirl the batter to coat the entire bottom. Cook for 1 to 2 minutes and turn. Cook another minute and transfer to a plate. Repeat until all the batter is used.

makes about 12 crepes

CHESTNUT CREAM AND VANILLA ICE CREAM

1 cup chestnut cream, found in specialty
    food shops (substitute Nutella or other
    nut spread if needed)

1 cup vanilla ice cream

Prepare the crepes and set aside. Spread ¼ cup of the chestnut cream in the center of each crepe, leaving about 1 inch around the edge. Fold over the top and bottom edges of the crepe, overlapping them by about ¼ inch. Fold the side edges to the center, creating a square. Place a scoop of vanilla ice cream in the center.

serves 4

BANANA-HONEY AND ALMOND

2 bananas, peeled and cut into ½-inch
    rounds

4 tablespoons honey
4 tablespoons slivered almonds

Prepare the crepes and set aside. Warm a nonstick skillet over medium heat. Place a crepe in the middle of the pan and spread evenly in the center half a sliced banana, drizzle with 1 tablespoon of honey, and sprinkle with 1 tablespoon of slivered almonds. Fold the edges to the center, overlapping them to cover the filling, creating a square. Cook for 1 minute and flip. Repeat to make 4 filled crepes. Serve warm.

serves 4

HAM AND CHEESE

4 thin slices mild ham
1 cup grated Emmental or Gruyère cheese

Prepare the crepes and set aside. Warm a skillet over medium heat. Place a crepe in the pan. Add a slice of ham in the center and sprinkle ¼ cup of cheese over the ham. Fold the edges of the crepe over the filling, overlapping them and creating a square. Cook for 1 to 2 minutes and flip. Cook another 1 or 2 minutes until the cheese is melted. Serve hot. Repeat to make 4 filled crepes.

serves 4

Chapter 4
CAFÉS AND BISTROS

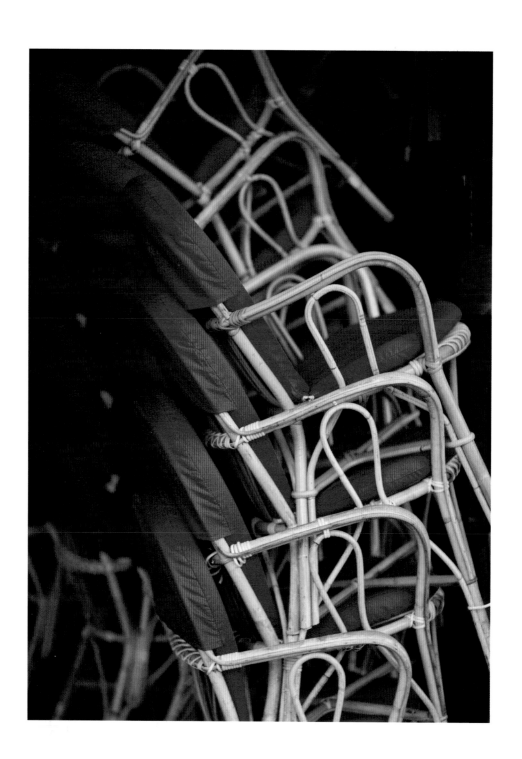

Assiette de Charcuterie
Charcuterie Plate

Croque Madame
Grilled Ham and Cheese Sandwich with Fried Egg

Salade Niçoise

Citron Pressé, Menthe, ou Grenadine à l'Eau
French Lemonade, Mint, or Grenadine Syrup with Water

Truites Grillées
Fresh Grilled Trout

Moules Marinières
Steamed Mussels

Poulet Frites
Roast Chicken with French Fries

Salade de Pommes de Terre à l'Oeuf Poché
Potato Salad with Poached Egg

Citrons Givrés
Sorbet-Filled Lemons

Tarte aux Noix et Amandes
Walnut and Almond Tart

Any café or bistro, in the tiniest country village to the bustling streets of any city, provided us with glimpses into the lives of locals: the postman stopping by for a quick coffee at the bar while on his morning route, traveling salesmen eating alone, workers having a drink at the bar at the end of their day. At the bistros, changing menus sported regional and local specialties for lunch, and sometimes the cafés had hot sandwiches. Savory salads with poached eggs and tender boiled potatoes or baked goat cheese with bitter salad greens and bacon are the salads we looked forward to, hopefully served with a charcuterie plate of pâté, *jambon cru*, and *saucisson*. For kids, of course, any version of a grilled cheese sandwich would do, and the French one, a *croque madame*, is laden with rich béchamel sauce and a fried egg. Drinks, ice creams, and tarts often finished the meal.

As a child I spent idle hours in cafés all across France people watching, and cafés are everywhere. The second we stepped off the plane into the sprawling corridors of Charles de Gaulle Airport, a brief stop at a café was in order—ham and butter sandwiches on baguettes, two Oranginas, and two coffees. The cigarette smoke hung in the air, the smell of perfume wafted from the duty-free shops, and the food and drinks were a stamp of arrival. As I munched my sandwich, slipping it from the cellophane wrapper, I watched people from every corner of the world coming and going. There were African women in flowing batik-printed gowns with luggage carts piled high with things to take home to families far away, and smart Parisian businessmen in tidy suits with briefcases. I could always tell the French stewardesses because they were elegantly dressed, little caps perched on top of their heads and Air France neck scarves perfectly knotted to the side.

My deepest memories of Paris are from days spent in the Jardin du Luxembourg and the rickety carousel that is still there, the iconic metal chairs out for anyone to enjoy, the crepe stand, the infinitely tall, leafy trees that line every pathway, a royal canopy shading a never-ending stream of people, tourists and residents, all sitting, drinking, reading, and watching one another. The café I loved the most was nestled under the trees, tables set out in the dusty, decomposed granite grounds, the bathroom down some stairs around the back, and at the bottom of the stairs a little old woman in a gray housecoat dusted with tiny pink and red flowers, her wispy white hair pulled back in a tight white bun. She was there to collect *centimes* (French pennies) from us. She wiped down the counters, offered us cloth towels to dry our hands, and smiled sweetly as I spoke to her in imperfect French, mumbling "*Merci, Madame.*" She seemed so old, older than my grandmothers.

As we left Paris and headed south, the cities became smaller and the cafés were more in the center of town, where moss-covered fountains gurgled up from stone ponds and the cool mist sprayed off the surface, giving relief from the heat. On early evening visits, my parents lingered at the table, sipping wine, with small dishes of peanuts or pistachios that were constantly refilled as my brother and I relished in the menu choices. More often than not I would have thick, syrupy *grenadine au limonade*, a pure sugar concoction of alleged pomegranate syrup (a good quarter cup worth and a cold bottle of clear lemon soda). My brother preferred the bright green mint flavor, a bit too much like toothpaste for my taste. These café visits or stops were never short, and we never protested, because we always had pockets full of new plastic soldiers or animal figurines, coloring books, and refills of whatever we were drinking. Sometimes, at cafés that were bistros as well, the visit would last so long it was time for dinner, so paper place mats were set, and cutlery and little glass cruets of oil, vinegar, and mustard appeared. *Entrecôte de boeuf, salade Niçoise,* and *poulet frites* were among the choices, and inevitably one of my parents would order something along the lines of kidneys in cream sauce or *gras-double* (tripe in tomato sauce). My brother, normally a very picky eater in California and a fan of white bread and bologna sandwiches, hot dogs, and American cheese, had no fear of the French menu, but he stuck to steak and French fries most days, followed by *crème caramel*.

—Ethel

The café experience was a must—you couldn't walk down any street in France without stumbling over the typical wicker café chairs and tables with silver-lined edges on every block. The little *épiceries* next to the cafés were a quick answer to the larger grocery chains if you needed a few extra necessities for dinner. I saw some amazing things—there were giant baskets of perfect porcini right on the sidewalk, like it was nothing! I consistently heard that Paris was an "assault on all the senses," which I think describes the café/bistro experience perfectly. Hearing orders shouted through the kitchen, people conversing in quick intonations, sugary and salty delights, the smell of delicious street food when we sat outside, and the smell of butter, chicken, meats, and cheeses when we sat inside, and most important, the comfort of having my mom or dad's arm around me when I sat close to them in the big bistro booths were all part of the experience.

I loved how the café/bistro was such a part of life, such a social thing, and at any time of day, especially during mealtime, each café seemed completely packed as if no one worked or time stood still. My sister and I would always order *grenadine au limonade* because nothing is more exciting than a bright red drink fizzing with sugary madness. Inside the cafés the small tile floors were often cracked and warped from decades of feet shuffling in and out of the social scene, and usually there were mirrors on the walls that showed years of wear and water stains. I was always scared to go to the restroom in cafés—it was a gamble to see if there was a "regular" toilet or a hole in porcelain on the ground between two footpads. Strangely enough, this was one of the things I remember so clearly about the cafés—the fear of the bathroom with a hole in the ground.

There was no need to rush when you were there—you often had to ask for the bill several times before the waiter in the perfectly pressed starched white apron brought it to you. It was like we entered a bubble where time slowed so significantly that you were forced to enjoy a few of the simple things in life—a good glass of wine and a good dose of people watching. As each man and woman passed by our table, I always tried to imagine what kind of life they experienced, what kind of stories they'd pass on, and even what they ate for breakfast. It was a dance of informal meetings every few seconds, again and again, with strangers. I was happy to be a part of these non-meetings, sipping my red drink, staining my white shirt.

—Sara

ASSIETTE DE CHARCUTERIE
Charcuterie Plate

Ahh, the prix fixe menu, written in white chalk on slate, the French script a bit hard to read but clear enough for me to know I had a choice of two. Charcuterie for the first course or snails. The choice was a difficult one, but either way I would be happy. A platter with slices of *saucisson sec* or rabbit rillettes, and hopefully a liver mousse pâté, plus rolled slices of *jambon cru*, all garnished with olives and cornichons, was always a sure bet. —Ethel

4 thick-cut slices prosciutto (⅓ pound)
Selection of salami-style cured meats
    (⅓ pound)
2-inch wedge of pâté, country or mousse
    or both

½ pint cornichon pickles
½ pint mixed olives
1 baguette, cut into ½-inch-thick rounds

Prepare a platter. Cut the prosciutto into 1-inch-thick strips crosswise and arrange on one section of the platter. Continue with precut salami slices or cut ¼-inch rounds from a whole salami and arrange on the platter along with the pâté. Either lay the pickles and olives alongside the meats or place in small bowls on the platter. Serve with the sliced baguette.

serves 4

CROQUE MADAME
Grilled Ham and Cheese Sandwich with Fried Egg

My first experience with a croque madame was at Genève-Plage, a water park in Geneva right on the border of France and Switzerland. One of our friends asked in broken English if I had ever tried one, and I shook my head curiously. She took my hand and led me to the little snack bodega next to the pool. We ordered, and I marveled at the cute egg on top—a very feminine sandwich.

—Sara

SAUCE

2 tablespoons unsalted butter

2 tablespoons all-purpose flour

1½ cups milk

¼ teaspoon salt

¼ teaspoon freshly grated nutmeg

SANDWICHES

2 tablespoons butter

4 slices pain de mie, challah, or other soft
   white bread

1 tablespoon Dijon-style mustard

4 thin slices boiled ham

2 thin slices Gruyère cheese

2 eggs

Preheat a broiler.

For the sauce, melt the butter in a saucepan over medium heat. When it has melted, remove it from the heat and stir in the flour to make a roux, or paste. Return to the heat and slowly whisk in the milk until smooth and blended, about 2 minutes. Add the salt and nutmeg. Continue to cook until it has thickened and the taste of flour is gone, about 15 minutes. Increase the heat if necessary to thicken. Set aside.

To make the sandwiches, butter one side of each piece of bread using 1 tablespoon of butter. Spread the mustard on the unbuttered sides of 2 of the slices. Layer the ham and cheese, then top with the remaining slices, butter side up.

Warm a skillet over medium-low heat, then cook the sandwiches for 3 minutes, until the bread is golden; turn and repeat on the other side. Place the cooked sandwiches on a baking sheet, spoon over about ½ cup of the sauce, and place under the broiler until the sauce is bubbling and golden, about 5 minutes. If you have extra sauce, you can freeze it for next time. While the sandwiches are in the oven quickly fry the eggs in the remaining 1 tablespoon of butter. Remove the sandwiches to two plates and top each with a fried egg.

makes 2 sandwiches

SALADE NIÇOISE

Today I think some version of the Niçoise salad is on most bistro and café menus, but at one time it was a regional specialty. The Niçoise packed in all of my favorite ingredients: Barely hard-boiled eggs with deep golden yellow yolks, salty anchovies, capers, and olives peppered over greens, all marinating in bitter green olive oil and red wine vinegar. It was a mélange far from home, not even a distant cousin to Howard Johnson's iceberg wedge with blue cheese dressing, which I also found delicious.

—Ethel

4 eggs

¼ pound French haricots verts or other small green beans, stem ends trimmed

6 small yellow, red, or white potatoes, peeled

2 tablespoons olive oil

½ teaspoon Dijon-style mustard

1 teaspoon red wine vinegar

¼ teaspoon sea salt

1 (5-ounce) can high-quality canned tuna, packed in olive oil, drained

3 ripe medium tomatoes, cut into 1-inch wedges

12 black, salt-, or olive oil–cured olives, pitted

6 fresh marinated anchovy fillets or oil-packed fillets, patted dry

1 teaspoon capers, drained and rinsed

Place the eggs in a small saucepan and cover with water. Over high heat, bring the water to a boil, turn off the heat, and let stand for 10 minutes. Remove the eggs from the pan and run them under cold water to halt the cooking. Once they have cooled enough to handle, peel them and cut them crosswise into ½-inch rounds.

Bring a large pot of water to a boil. Fill a large bowl of water with ice cubes and set aside. Slip the beans into the boiling water and cook for about 3 minutes. Using a slotted spoon, remove the beans from the water and transfer them to the ice water. Return the water to a boil and cook the potatoes until tender and easily pierced with the tines of a fork, about 15 minutes. Drain the potatoes and allow to cool, then cut into halves. Remove the beans from the ice water and pat dry.

In a large bowl, whisk together the olive oil, mustard, vinegar, and salt. Add the tuna, tomatoes, potatoes, and beans and gently toss together. Add the olives, anchovies, capers, and eggs, gently fold into the salad, and serve.

serves 4

CITRON PRESSÉ, MENTHE, OU GRENADINE À L'EAU

French Lemonade, Mint,
or Grenadine Syrup with Water

Cafés in France are for people of all ages and all walks of life: a quick coffee on your way to work or the grocery store, several hours reading quietly alone, or an afternoon spent with friends and family. As a child, the excitement came from a special drink. In California it was the Shirley Temple, served in a dimpled plastic glass with, hopefully, two maraschino cherries at the bottom. In France it was sweet grenadine or mint syrup two inches deep, a stir stick, and my own personal pitcher of chilled water. The trick was to fill the glass with water, then refill it every time it dropped an inch, making the drink last as long as possible.   —Ethel

½ cup freshly squeezed lemon juice   ¼ cup sugar
Pitcher of chilled water   Grenadine syrup or mint syrup

Put ¼ cup of freshly squeezed lemon juice in each of two glasses with a pitcher of chilled water and a dish of sugar on the side. Mix together until sweetened to one's liking.

For the Grenadine and *Menthe à l'Eau*, pour ¼ cup or less of the syrup, depending on desired sweetness, into two tall glasses and add cold water as needed. Stir and enjoy.

serves 2

TRUITES GRILLÉES
Fresh Grilled Trout

Hôtel Relais Notre Dame, in the lakeside village of Quinson, is not actually on the lake; its terrace overlooks a wheat field flanked by vineyards. The owners, a brother and sister, have a fish tank off to the side and behind the kitchen, a large one filled with eight- to ten-inch-long trout. If you order *le plat Truite Amandine*, you get to choose your fish. To do so, you need to run quickly and carefully across the road, as the terrace is separated from the hotel and restaurant by a busy road. However, in my child's mind, the restaurant did not overlook a wheat field, but the lake and the tank were just outside the terrace wall also overlooking the lake. I am always surprised when we return that my dusky view is not rippling pools but golden-topped grain stalks, violet from the sunset. I was sure this restaurant was on the water.

—Ethel

2 whole fresh trout, cleaned, scales removed

2 tablespoons extra-virgin olive oil

1 tablespoon coarse sea salt

2 whole lemons

6 sprigs fresh thyme

1 tablespoon canola or other vegetable oil for the grill

Prepare a charcoal grill or heat a gas grill to medium-high temperature.

Rinse the fish and pat dry. Rub the fish all over with the olive oil and salt. Cut one of the lemons crosswise into ½-inch slices. Divide the lemon slices between the 2 fish, lining their insides. Lay the fresh thyme on top of the lemons. Rub the fish all over with the olive oil and salt.

Brush the grill with the canola oil and place the fish on the grill. Cook until the fish pulls easily from the grill, about 6 minutes; turn and cook the other side. If it sticks let it cook another 2 minutes and then turn. Cook another 6 to 8 minutes—the fish should be firm to the touch.

serves 2 to 4 (1 fish per person or ½ fillet)

MOULES MARINIÈRES
Steamed Mussels

Up until the time I was ten years old or so, before there were any supermarkets in the villages near our house, we bought our fish from "the fish man." When we heard him honk on Wednesday afternoon, we'd run out the front door and find him there on the narrow road, flinging up the sides of his gray van to display big trays full of crushed ice spread with neatly arranged fish. Whenever he had mussels, my mom and Marie bought them, and we cooked them together in Marie's kitchen in a big pot, adding the wild thyme that Aileen and I had gathered, along with fresh bay leaves from the neighbors down the road. The kitchen aroma wafted though the whole house, and I could hardly wait to dip my bread in the broth and to pick the plump orange mussels from their shells with my fork.

—Ethel

1 tablespoon extra-virgin olive oil	1 cup dry white wine
1 tablespoon unsalted butter	1 teaspoon fresh thyme leaves or several
½ yellow onion, chopped	sprigs
5 pounds mussels, scrubbed and debearded	1 bay leaf
if necessary	3 cloves garlic

In the bottom of a large pot, combine the olive oil and butter and place over medium-high heat until the butter foams. Add the onion and sauté until translucent, 2 to 3 minutes. Add the mussels and pour in the wine. Rub the thyme between your hands over the pot, allowing it to fall over the mussels. Add the bay leaf and then grate the garlic over the mussels. Cover, lower the heat to low, and cook just until the mussels open, 10 to 12 minutes. Uncover the pot and turn the mussels in the broth. Using a large slotted spoon, scoop the mussels into individual bowls, discarding any that failed to open. Ladle a little broth into each bowl and serve at once.

serves 4

POULET FRITES
Roast Chicken with French Fries

"Poulet frites!" I'd yell every time we went to a restaurant. My parents would look at the menu, discuss the different possibilities, and then decide to be adventuresome. I, on the other hand, always knew exactly what I wanted—delicious crisp chicken and a heaping mound of thin French fries, crunchy on the outside, soft on the inside, served with the rich, creamy mayonnaise that tasted nothing like home.

—Sara

1 (3½-pound) chicken, cut into quarters
2 cloves garlic, peeled and lightly crushed
2 tablespoons extra-virgin olive oil
1 to 1 ½ tablespoons sea salt
2 tablespoons unsalted butter

FRITES

4 large russet or Kennebec potatoes
Canola oil or other vegetable oil for
   deep-frying
1 teaspoon salt

Preheat the oven to 400°F.

Rub the chicken quarters all over with the garlic. Place the pieces, skin side up, on a baking sheet. Rub them all over with olive oil followed by the salt. Bake for about 20 minutes, then using a butter knife, spread 1 tablespoon of the butter over the tops of the chicken pieces. Continue to cook, basting once more with the remaining 1 tablespoon of butter. Cook the chicken until the juices run clear when pierced with a knife, about 1 hour.

While the chicken is cooking, prepare the French fries. Peel the potatoes and trim them to make a rectangular block. Cut the potatoes evenly into batons or sticks ¼ inch wide by ¼ inch thick. Place in cold water and continue to change the water until it is clear. Dry the potatoes completely with a towel.

In a deep fryer or a Dutch oven fitted with a candy thermometer, heat the oil over medium heat until it reaches 325°F. Add the potatoes, only a few handfuls at a time, being sure not to overcrowd them. Increase the heat to medium-high and fry until the potatoes have formed a skin and are faintly golden, 6 to 7 minutes. Remove to a paper towel–lined platter. Repeat until all are cooked. Let rest for 15 minutes to 2 hours before the second frying.

When ready to serve, heat the oil again to 350°F. Fry the potatoes in handfuls as before until they turn a warm golden brown, about 5 minutes. Sprinkle with salt.

serves 4

SALADE DE POMMES DE TERRE À L'OEUF POCHÉ
Potato Salad with Poached Egg

I'm sure I had this many times when I was a kid, but my best memory of this salad was a few years ago, when I randomly happened upon an adorable café in the thirteenth arrondissement that was completely empty. I picked the café for no other reason than it was the closest one near the apartment I was staying in, it looked comfortable, and it had that traditional, almost clichéd French look I couldn't resist. Five minutes after ordering, I was delivered the most beautiful lettuce I'd ever seen, bright green, strong, and sculptural, with what looked like hand-painted radicchio. I felt like a culinary artist as my fork sliced into the eggs, mixing the yellow with the green and bits of purple. I chomped down on the crunchy fresh lettuce; the sound made a symphony with the sounds of the city: the click of high heels on the sidewalk, French children just out of school laughing and running, and the bustle of motor scooters on the busy Parisian streets.

—Sara

1 small head butter lettuce

1 head radicchio

8 new white, red, or yellow potatoes, peeled

4 (1-inch-thick) slices rustic country bread

5 tablespoons extra-virgin olive oil

1 clove garlic, peeled and lightly crushed

1 tablespoon champagne vinegar

½ teaspoon Dijon-style mustard

1 teaspoon finely minced shallot

½ teaspoon coarse sea salt

¼ teaspoon freshly ground black pepper

1 tablespoon fresh tarragon leaves

1 tablespoon coarsely chopped fresh Italian parsley leaves

4 fresh eggs

1 clove garlic, peeled

Preheat the oven to 350°F.

Remove the leaves from the lettuce and the radicchio and discard any tough or damaged leaves. Trim the stems and tear the greens into 2-inch pieces. Wash and dry with a salad spinner or pat the leaves dry after washing with a clean dish towel.

Place the potatoes on a steamer rack in a saucepan with at least 1 inch of water. Cover and bring the water to a boil over medium heat. Cook the potatoes, adding more water if needed as it evaporates, until fork-tender, about 15 minutes. Set the potatoes aside to cool, then cut into halves.

Brush all sides of the bread slices with 2 tablespoons of the olive oil and rub all sides with the crushed clove of garlic. Place on a baking sheet and cook for 3 to 4 minutes in the oven, until brown. Turn and cook another 3 to 4 minutes, then remove from the oven.

In a large bowl, whisk together the remaining 3 tablespoons of olive oil, the champagne vinegar, mustard, shallot, and half of the salt and pepper. Add the salad greens, tarragon, and parsley. Do not toss together until ready to serve.

Bring a large skillet filled with water to a boil over medium heat. Crack the eggs, one at a time, into a small bowl and gently slip each into the water. To cook the tops of the eggs, gently spoon water over the tops several times and cook for 3 to 4 minutes.

Add the cooled potatoes to the salad and toss to coat. Divide the salad equally among four dinner plates and using a slotted spoon, remove the eggs from the poaching water and place one on top of each salad. Sprinkle the eggs with the remaining salt and pepper, and serve each salad with a slice of toast.

serves 4

CITRONS GIVRÉS
Sorbet-Filled Lemons

The glossy plastic laminated menu boards parked out front most cafés sent our ice cream–obsessed minds spinning, and if it was on a bistro menu it meant it would be a choice for dessert. Mikado, Cornet, and Magnum bars, just to name a few, swirled on the Day-Glo menus, ready to be pulled from the freezer below and placed in our hands. Occasionally a café would have something special on the board: frozen, hollowed-out lemons and oranges filled with sorbet and capped with the stem end of the fruit rind. Next to push-up Popsicles this was haute cuisine, and its elegance and sophistication seemed out of place on the menu board.

—Ethel

8 lemons

1 cup sugar

1 tablespoon vodka

To prepare the lemons, cut a quarter off the stem end. At the opposite end, cut just a thin slice through the rind only from the bottom, not cutting through to the fruit. This will keep the lemon level when serving. From the stem end trim away any fruit, leaving a small yellow "cap" about the size of a quarter and set aside.

Using a spoon, gently scoop the flesh from the lemons. Place the hollowed-out lemons upright on their stem ends on a baking sheet and put into the freezer.

Using your hands, squeeze the removed pulp to extract the juice and pass it through a fine-mesh sieve. You will need 1 cup of juice.

In a saucepan, stir together 1 cup water and the sugar, and cook over medium heat until the sugar is completely dissolved. Place in the refrigerator and let cool for at least 1 hour and up to 24 hours. Stir in the cup of lemon juice and the vodka. Pour into a baking dish large enough to hold the liquid and freeze for 24 hours. Alternatively, process the sorbet in an ice cream maker according to the manufacturer's instructions. Fill each chilled, hollowed lemon with the sorbet, top with a "cap," and place in the freezer to chill for at least 2 hours and up to 1 week.

serves 8

TARTE AUX NOIX ET AMANDES
Walnut and Almond Tart

The flaky pastry crumbled under my fork and the sweetness of the sugar-coated toasted walnuts and almonds reminded me of my grandmother's pecan pie, though not as sweet and sticky but more fragrant and salty. It must have been the butter. Although usually a winter dessert, occasionally this nut tart pops up in early summer before stone fruits have exploded onto the market. Once we bought a whole one, and I ate it for three meals a day until all that was left were sticky nut crumbs stuck to the cardboard pastry round.   —Ethel

PASTRY

1½ cups all-purpose flour

¼ cup granulated sugar

½ cup unsalted butter, cut into ½-inch chunks

1 large egg

FILLING

2 tablespoons butter, melted and cooled

½ cup firmly packed light brown sugar

2 large eggs

½ cup Cointreau

One 1-inch piece of vanilla bean

1½ cups walnuts and almonds, lightly toasted

Preheat the oven to 350°F.

To make the pastry, stir together the flour and granulated sugar. Add the butter and work it in with your fingertips until the mixture becomes crumblike. Add the egg and mix it with a fork. Tightly pack the dough into a ball. Press the dough evenly into a 10-inch tart pan with a removable bottom. Refrigerate until ready to use.

To make the filling, combine the melted butter, brown sugar, eggs, Cointreau, and vanilla. Beat until well blended. Stir in the nuts and pour the filling into the tart pan. Do not overfill.

Bake until the crust and the filling are golden brown, about 50 minutes. Transfer to a rack to cool. Remove the pan rim and slide the tart onto a plate. Serve warm or at room temperature.

serves 8 to 10

Chapter 5

AFTERNOON SNACKS
(GOÛTER)

Pain au Chocolat
Chocolate Bar Sandwiches

Sandwiches aux Tomates
Tomato and Olive Oil Sandwiches

Pâte à Tartiner au Chocolat et aux Noisettes
Chocolate-Hazelnut Spread

Madeleines

Fromage Blanc avec Confiture de Prunes
Farmer's Cheese with Plum Preserves

Gougères
Savory Puff Pastry

Late afternoon, with dinner still hours away, was the peak of play-time for us, our energy fueled by our *goûter*, the French word for late afternoon snacks, a treat reserved for children, not always healthy, often a version of bread and chocolate. As we spent ample time with family and friends, most with children of varying ages, we also jumped in on the fun and were fed, alongside our friends, tomato and olive oil sandwiches, chocolate hazelnut spread on open-faced baguette sandwiches, moist vanilla-scented madeleine cakes, and more.

A mix of sweet and savory snacks midday were sure to carry us to the aperitif hour in the early evening, when the drinks, olives, and salted nuts would segue into a long multi-course dinner with the grown-ups, including some lush dessert, but until then, goûter was the meal and we were refueled and sent back out to play.

Hot lazy summers were familiar to me in both California and Provence. By four in the afternoon the sun would still hang high and pesky little flies would relentlessly land on our arms and legs, attracted by our salted skin. Regardless of whether we were in France or California, most of my summer days were spent seeking relief from the dry heat through shade or water. France was special, though, because we lived in the country, not in town like at home. The fields, vineyards, and hillsides were our playgrounds. We had such freedom—out the door in the morning, down tractor roads, making bows and arrows from mulberry branches and baling twine, and excavating Roman tiles and even dinosaur bones. Around noon, we all headed home for lunch and a nap, and then at three we were back out the door. On days when no body of water was at hand, my friend Aileen, my brother, and I pitched beach umbrellas in the overgrown grassy meadows, laid out soft French quilts, and prayed for a thunderstorm to break the heat that hummed with the sounds of crickets and cicadas. Somebody's mother would eventually track us down and bring us *goûter*. Dinner wouldn't be served until at least eight or nine in the evening, so afternoon sustenance was essential. The snacks varied from day to day, but usually were served in the form of tomato and olive oil sandwiches, yogurts, sweet baguette and chocolate bar sandwiches, sometimes spread with butter. My very favorites, however, were dense little madeleine cakes, baked in the shape of small boats, all washed down with Orangina, a light orange soda made with fruit juice.

—Ethel

Everything about snack time reminds me of swimming: running barefoot from the pool *sans* towel with my sister, water still dripping down my legs, tufts of thick crabgrass itching the bottom of my feet, to the wood table on the right side of the stone house. By the time I would arrive, the treats would be neatly laid out for us kids—slices of bread with Nutella and honey, jam, cheese, and a possible bonus candy bar. When we were done, my bathing suit would be mostly dry from the August heat. Not knowing the language perfectly, I always felt like a bit of an outsider with the other French kids. However, I would communicate my humor by smearing chocolate spread all over my mouth and face, trying to extend my tongue so far to lick off every bit from the tip of my nose to underneath my chin; sticking my hands in the jar of honey and trying to wipe the sticky sweetness all over my sister's arms; shoving as many pieces of chocolate in my mouth as I could while trying to speak a sentence without the chocolate falling out—all hilarious and annoying.

—Sara

PAIN AU CHOCOLAT
Chocolate Bar Sandwiches

As soon as my friend Aileen would arrive home from school, which goes well into July in France, I would hurry over to her house for a long, late afternoon of running through the fields, playing house in little, stone, hunting cabins, or playing dress-up from my mother's chest of 1950s prom dresses and my grandmother's cocktail gowns. Aileen's mother, Marie, would load us up with fresh lengths of baguette filled with squares of dark or milk chocolate. I have never even tried to re-create this delectable snack at home in the United States because nothing can compare, not the chocolate, the butter, or the bread, but this is a good facsimile. Now, my sons are served a similar snack by their grandmother, *Mamie* Paulette, but the bread is a sweet *pain au lait* roll.

—Ethel

2 (3- to 4-ounce) bars semisweet or milk chocolate

1 teaspoon unsalted butter (optional)

1 fresh, sweet baguette, not sour dough, cut crosswise into quarters

Break the chocolate into pieces, spread the butter, if using, on the insides of the bread, and layer with the chocolate squares.

serves 4

SANDWICHES AUX TOMATES
Tomato and Olive Oil Sandwiches

Marie and her family always lived on our country road in Fox-Amphoux, and I have known them my entire life. Marie, in expected Italian fashion (she was originally from Calabria), would insist that we eat whenever we were at her home. I spent many afternoons in her living room with her daughter Aileen. We would watch American soap operas dubbed in French and pore over teen magazines filled with the tacky glamour of Riviera pop stars and actors. Her father would pick peaches and tomatoes from the garden, one to be eaten alongside the other. If we made it home before finishing off the harvest, Marie would slice open a baguette, drizzle it with dark green bitter olive oil, add several thick slices of tomato, and sprinkle with salt.

—Ethel

1 baguette

4 tablespoons extra-virgin olive oil

3 large ripe tomatoes, cores removed and cut into ¼-inch-thick slices

1 teaspoon coarse sea salt

Cut the baguette into 4 equal lengths, slicing them open to create sandwiches. Drizzle 1 tablespoon of olive oil on the open slices of each sandwich, layer with the tomato slices, and sprinkle each with sea salt.

serves 4

PÂTE À TARTINER AU CHOCOLAT ET AUX NOISETTES
Chocolate-Hazelnut Spread

Swimming always made me hungry, hungrier than I usually was at snack time. When the *goûter* was ready, we had been in the pool for at least four hours on any given day. My parents' friends' kids, my sister, and I would eat barefoot at the picnic table, and there was a plethora of snacks for us to enjoy, including bread and chocolate spread. There was a mad dash for the chocolate, and all the kids had chocolate covering their faces, legs, and fingers. There was so much excited chattering, overlapping of French kids' words, one sentence flowing into the next, that I had no idea what anyone was saying. I did have a feeling that they were discussing how to properly spread the chocolate on the bread or eat the chocolate: "No, no, no, do it like THIS; you need much more ..." There was usually a big, hairy dog sitting next to the table, furiously panting from the heat, waiting patiently for scraps to fall on the ground. We sat on the table, legs dangling over the side, looking out into the beautiful distant mountains of the Luberon and licking our fingers clean.

—Sara

1 pound shelled hazelnuts

2 tablespoons honey

1 teaspoon pure vanilla extract

¼ teaspoon salt

6 ounces bittersweet chocolate, melted

¼ cup canola or other light vegetable oil

Sweet baguette, not sourdough, for serving

Preheat the oven to 300°F.

Spread the hazelnuts on a baking sheet and place in the oven. Toast for 8 to 10 minutes, turning often to prevent browning.

Remove the hazelnuts from the oven and let cool until able to handle. Take a handful of the nuts in your hand and rub to remove the skins. The skins will not completely come off. Place in the bowl of a food processor fitted with a metal blade and process the nuts until they form a smooth paste.

With the food processor running slowly, add the honey, vanilla, salt, melted chocolate, and oil. Process until smooth and transfer to ½-pint jars; it will keep in the refrigerator for up to 3 months. Serve on slices of sweet baguette.

makes 1 pint

MADELEINES

Madeleines are the tea cakes of France, known by their iconic shape of a small fluted-bottom boat, immortalized in French literature by Marcel Proust. Thankfully they are available everywhere. Fresh baked from the boulangerie is best, but much less precious and equally delicious are the industrial madeleines, sold in large bags. I was addicted to the sweet, pound cake–like boats; a stickiness coated each little cake, clinging to my fingers, leaving me smelling of vanilla, eggs, and butter. Like me, my own children are not discriminating and love the ones from store-bought bags as much as I do, and I can still munch away, two for them and one for me.

—Ethel

Butter, for greasing the madeleine pans

1½ cups all-purpose flour

½ teaspoon baking powder

¼ teaspoon salt

¾ cup (1½ sticks) unsalted butter, cut into
   ½-inch pieces

3 eggs

1 egg yolk

¾ cup sugar

1½ teaspoons pure vanilla extract

Preheat the oven to 450°F.

Generously grease two 12-count madeleine pans with butter and set aside.

In a medium bowl, sift together the flour, baking powder, and salt.

In another small bowl, mash the butter, using a spatula, until smooth and creamy.

In a third medium bowl, combine the eggs, egg yolk, sugar, and vanilla and beat together on high speed, using an electric mixer, until smooth and pale yellow. Using a rubber spatula, gently fold the flour mixture into the egg batter until incorporated. Fold ½ cup of the batter into the creamed butter and then add the butter mixture to the remaining batter. Gently mix until smooth and light in texture. Let the batter rest for 30 to 40 minutes.

Fill each mold three-quarters full to allow for rising. Place in the oven and bake until the madeleines are just golden brown around the edges and on the tops, just 7 to 8 minutes. Remove from the oven while still hot, gently loosen from the molds with a knife, and transfer to a rack to cool.

makes 24

FROMAGE BLANC AVEC CONFITURE DE PRUNES
Farmer's Cheese with Plum Preserves

The dairy section of any French grocery store is like nothing I have ever experienced. There are yogurts in every flavor, from chestnut to wild plum, and *petit-suisse*, something like a blend of sour cream and cream cheese, packaged in extra-small yogurt pots. As a child, I remember that when I slipped the *petit-suisse* into the bowl it came out of the package wrapped in paper, which I picked off. Next, it needed to be sweetened with sugar, honey, jam, or even chocolate powder. *Fromage blanc*, another mysterious treat, a cross between yogurt and soft cheese, is mild and creamy and was always served to me in a small earthenware bowl topped with sweet, aromatic black plum preserves. Here is a simple way to make a *fromage blanc* at home using lemon juice to curdle the milk. Once the milk curdles, the whey is drained off and the cheese is ready. The texture is somewhat grainy but can be smoothed out by adding a bit of cream.

—Ethel

2 quarts whole milk

½ teaspoon salt

2 tablespoons freshly squeezed and strained lemon juice

2 cups buttermilk

1 tablespoon whipping cream (optional)

¾ cup plum preserves or other favorite jam

In a large saucepan over medium heat, warm the milk and stir in the salt. Just as it begins to bubble on the sides, remove from the heat and stir in the lemon juice and buttermilk. The curds and whey will begin to separate. Let stand for 10 to 15 minutes.

While the mixture is resting, line a colander with a clean dishcloth or double layer of cheesecloth. Place the colander over a bowl, making sure there is room in the bowl for the whey to collect. Pour the curds into the colander and let drain for about 30 minutes. Discard the whey. Wrap the edges of the cloth up around the curds and tie off with kitchen twine. Let the cheese drain, keeping the bundle in the cheesecloth for 1 hour or longer for a firmer cheese. The cheese will have the texture of a crumbly cottage cheese, a little bit drier.

For a softer, creamier cheese, transfer the fromage blanc to a bowl and gently stir in the whipping cream, if using.

To serve, spoon ½ cup of the cheese into a bowl and top with 2 tablespoons of the plum preserves.

makes 2 cups cheese, serves 4

GOUGÈRES
Savory Puff Pastry

Gougères are made by folding strong Gruyère cheese into a classic cream puff pastry dough, pâte à choux. Once baked, the bite-sized puffs are light, flavorful, and better than any cracker with cheese. At the bakery, when buying fresh bread in the morning, my brother and I were each allowed to choose afternoon snacks. I would get a half dozen *gougères* in a paper bag and save them on the kitchen counter until *goûter*. Then, once released from rest time, I would rush down the stone and tile stairs into the cool dark kitchen, grab my treats and head out to the shade of the mulberry trees with whatever book I was reading at the time tucked under my arm.

—Ethel

6 tablespoons unsalted butter
1 teaspoon salt
½ teaspoon freshly ground white pepper
1 cup all-purpose flour

4 large eggs
1½ cups grated Gruyère cheese
1 tablespoon water, lightly beaten with 1 egg
   (egg wash)

Preheat the oven to 425°F.

In a large saucepan over medium-high heat, combine 1 cup water, the butter, salt, and pepper. Bring to a boil, stirring, until the butter has completely melted, 2 to 3 minutes. Put the flour in all at once, and mix vigorously with a wooden spoon until a thick paste forms and pulls away from the side of the pan, about 3 minutes. Remove from the heat and make a well in the center. Crack 1 egg into the well and beat it into the hot mixture, either with the wooden spoon or an electric handheld mixer, until well incorporated. Repeat with the remaining 3 eggs, one at a time. Whisk in 1 cup of the cheese, mixing well.

Line two baking sheets with nonstick mats or parchment paper.

Use a teaspoon to shape the *gougères*. Dip the spoon into a glass of cold water, then scoop up a generous teaspoon of the mixture and push it onto the baking sheet with your fingertips. Repeat, dipping the spoon in the water each time to prevent sticking. When done, brush the top of each with a little of the egg mixture and sprinkle with a little of the remaining ½ cup of cheese.

Bake for 10 minutes, then reduce the heat to 350°F and bake until the gougères are golden brown and crunchy, about 15 minutes. If underdone, they will be mushy and undercooked inside. When done, vent the gougères by piercing each with a wooden skewer, then turn off the oven. Leave them in the oven for 10 minutes. Serve warm or at room temperature.

makes 30, serves 6 to 8

Chapter 6
MEALS WITH FAMILY AND FRIENDS

SARDINES GRILLÉES
Grilled Sardines

CÔTES D'AGNEAU GRILLÉES AU ROMARIN
Rosemary Grilled Lamb Chops

SOUPE DE POISSON
Provençal Fish Soup

LE GRAND AÏOLI
Aïoli with Vegetables and Salted Cod

BROUILLADE AUX TRUFFES
Truffled Eggs

MELON AU JAMBON CRU
Prosciutto-Wrapped Melon

LAPIN AUX CAROTTES, OIGNONS, ET POMMES DE TERRE
Braised Rabbit with Carrots, Onions, and Potatoes

ESCARGOTS
Snails in Garlic Butter

BOUCHÉES À LA REINE
Puff Pastry Shells Filled with Chanterelles and Chicken

DAUBE
Beef Stew

RÔTI DE PORC ET SAUCE AUX CÈPES
Roast Pork Loin with Rosemary and Porcini Mushrooms

GNOCCHI À LA BOLOGNAISE
Potato Dumplings with Bolognese Sauce

ÎLES FLOTTANTES
Poached Meringues in Crème Anglaise

ROSES DES SABLES
Chocolate Cornflake Treats

At the end of each day and certainly following on the heels of the earlier days of the holiday, the long road trip behind us, mornings we strolled through the *marchés*, lunch and afternoons we spent sampling street food, or in cafés and bistros, and we recharged our energy with late afternoon *goûter* chocolate-filled treats. The days subsided into the lingering and food-centered evenings, often spent outside under a canopy of mulberry trees or the stunning star-filled skies of Provence. Those evenings we sampled snails in garlic sauce, fresh grilled sardines, and bite-sized lamb chops. Other evenings, if a chill hit the air, meals were moved inside and were richer collections of warming beef *daube*, baked *bouchée à la reine* pastry shells filled with chicken and mushrooms, bowls of rich Provençal fish stew, and always a dessert, preferably something along the lines of *îles flottantes*, clouds of meringue served in bowls of *crème anglaise* custard.

Anyone who has ever been to France and had the pleasure of being invited to someone's home for a meal, lunch or dinner, knows well how long this epic process can take, unless it's in the middle of a workday, in which case just budget for 2½ hours. I loved such meals: a party every time, on arrival an aperitif table, the best invention ever! Drink choices were from collections of bottles, some homemade sweet wines; thyme, quince, cherry, and walnut were not for me, though. I was offered grenadine, sometimes sickeningly sweet orange Fanta soda, a bowl of ice, and snacks—salami, peanuts, pistachios, olives, cornichons, and bite-sized pizza crackers (I still bring boxes of these home to the States). The aperitifs take at least an hour, an hour of playtime for the kids and a moment of adult connection for parents; next, *le repas*, dinner! I was fascinated by the world of adults, and as I was usually the oldest child at most dinners, I relished sitting with the adults, showing off my adventurous eating, hanging on every word and story, trying to follow incomprehensible discussions in French about local politics, but mostly interested in any gossipy tidbits that slipped out.

The younger children, my brother, and any others collected for the evening slowly slipped from their chairs as evenings carried on, eventually ending up under the table playing with whatever toys were handy. I, however, stayed and was often privy to lengthy and unbelievable stories about World War II: tales of midnight escapes from trains bound for Germany, or of Nazi soldiers that supposedly lived in our house during the occupation and of women who worked the fields while the men fought in the resistance. I was in awe of such vivid stories of generations past and couldn't believe I was allowed to sit up late under the summer night stars listening and having my questions answered.

Dessert always showed up around this time, custard and fruit tarts, ice cream, and, if we were really lucky, an amazing French creation, *îles flottantes*. Just as the name implies, they are soft billowy mounds of poached meringue floating in delicate vanilla-infused crème anglaise, which of course, in France you can buy in the dairy section of any grocery store! And yes, as the name implies, it really does float and can be nudged from one side of the dish to the other. Testing the credulity of the name cannot be considered playing with your food.

—Ethel

My sister and I hid in the tall grass, bugs flying in our ears, as we tried to avoid them by shutting our eyes and waving our hands next to our heads. We heard the expected "*À table!*" from one of the adults in the house up the hill, echoing throughout the field we played in. Dinner—eating, drinking with family, rosé on a cool summer evening. It was okay to drink a little wine with your parents at the table—it was accepted as a sort of rite of passage for French kids. It was a part of life.

Days were organized around mealtime. Each day was a simple culinary adventure, easy, light, and happy: salad, melon, cheese, meats, yogurt, and wine. Then, after swimming, hiking, or *goûter*, dinner was ready (never before 8:00 PM) and we got down with the heavy stuff. I loved the sound of the crickets as we ate, and if we were so lucky, we were graced with fireflies at dusk—my nighttime friends.

I couldn't stand sitting still—I thought adults were boring and had no idea why anyone would sit and talk at a table for hours. I had better things to do and just wanted to skip to dessert. Usually there were other children at the table who were equally antsy to run and play, so I had partners in crime: We had to leave the table NOW. With our bellies full of the last course, which was usually cheese or yogurt, we ran to play in one of the kid's rooms. They taught my sister and me naughty French words; we taught them equally bad English words. We dressed up, put on plays, read *Tintin* in French and in English, and worked off the pent-up energy accumulated from two hours at the table. All that said, the table, regardless of how stagnant and boring it was to a child, was and always will be the heart and life of the home and our collective memories.

—Sara

SARDINES GRILLÉES
Grilled Sardines

Well, the first time I ever had a fresh grilled sardine was in France, because in California sardines were canned or fish bait. I do love canned sardines, especially served up on crackers with a dollop of cream cheese, but fresh grilled sardines, laden with olive oil and salt, are hardly the same food. As fresh sardines from the market, a grocery bag full, were prepared, we would wander down the narrow country lane, counting the glowworms clinging to the rocky retaining walls, the sounds of bats and owls echoing through the oak trees. We played night tag in the vineyards until we were called to dinner, and when we arrived the grill was already sizzling hot, and grown-ups were drinking *pastis*.

—Ethel

16 to 20 fresh sardines, each about 7 inches
    long, cleaned
⅓ cup extra-virgin olive oil

1 teaspoon coarse sea salt
½ teaspoon freshly ground black pepper
2 lemons, thinly sliced

Prepare a charcoal grill to a high heat.

Wash the sardines inside and out and pat dry with paper towels. Place them in a shallow baking dish, drizzle with ¼ cup of the olive oil, and sprinkle all over with the salt and pepper. Let stand for 10 to 15 minutes.

When the coals are ready, baste the grill with the remaining olive oil. Place the sardines on the grill rack and cook until the skin is crisp and golden, about 5 minutes. Using a spatula, gently turn the sardines and cook on the other side. If they lift easily, they are ready to turn. If they stick, cook another minute or so. Once turned, cook another 5 minutes.

Transfer to a platter and garnish with a bit of salt and the lemon slices.

serves 4 to 6

CÔTES D'AGNEAU GRILLÉES AU ROMARIN
Rosemary Grilled Lamb Chops

I always loved the abundant rosemary bushes in Provence. It was and still is a tradition as I walk by to grab a pinch, squeezing between my thumb and index finger, releasing those amazing aromatic scents—it reminded me of fresh baked bread in small towns. It's a funny comparison, but the experience of eating lamb was similar to that of eating a Tootsie pop—the closer I got to the center, the more delicious things became. The closer the meat was to the bone, the more succulent and tasty it was. The smell of the rosemary was so strong; it brought me back to hiking in the mountains in the south, where, when the wind picked up, it smelled like a twenty-four-hour rosemary feast.

—Sara

8 rib lamb chops

1 teaspoon coarse sea salt

1 teaspoon freshly ground black pepper

2 tablespoons extra-virgin olive oil

8 sprigs fresh rosemary, about 4 inches long

Preheat a charcoal grill to a high temperature.

In a large bowl, toss together the lamp chops, salt, pepper, olive oil, and rosemary sprigs. Let stand for 10 to 15 minutes. Lay the lamb chops on the hot grill and cook 3 minutes on each side for rare, 5 minutes on each side for medium. Remove and serve immediately with a green salad.

serves 8

SOUPE DE POISSON
Provençal Fish Soup

My mom, always adventurous and creative, was determined to re-create in California so much of what we experienced in France. If someone was butchering a pig, she was there collecting the blood to make *boudin* sausage. She'd hunt in Mexican grocery stores for sweetbreads to sauté in butter and garlic. Mimicking our time on the coast of Marseille, we once took a trip to the California north coast, Salt Point, where we fished for rockfish, gathered mussels, and unloaded the food mill from the car to make Provençal fish soup over an open fire.

—Ethel

ROUILLE

2 teaspoons crushed dried chile, seeds removed

6 to 8 cloves garlic, coarsely chopped

¼ teaspoon coarse sea salt

1 tablespoon fresh bread crumbs

½ teaspoon saffron threads soaked in 1 tablespoon boiling water

2 egg yolks, at room temperature

½ to ¾ cup extra-virgin olive oil

FISH STOCK

2 tablespoons extra-virgin olive oil

1 large yellow onion, quartered through the stem end

2 cloves garlic, crushed or sliced

2 carrots, peeled and cut into 3 or 4 pieces

1 leek, separated into white and green parts, each part cut into 2 or 3 pieces

2 pounds fish heads from non-oily fish, such as sea bass, monkfish, snapper, cod, or sole

3 to 4 sprigs fresh Italian flat-leaf parsley

3 to 4 sprigs fresh thyme

8 black peppercorns

1 ½ cups dry white wine

SOUP

6 tablespoons extra-virgin olive oil

1 pound mixed rockfish, such as snapper

3 cloves garlic

2 medium yellow onions, quartered

4 potatoes, sliced ½ inch thick

2 bay leaves

6 sprigs fresh thyme

6 large ripe tomatoes

4 cups Fish Stock

4 pieces fennel stalk

½ teaspoon coarse sea salt

½ teaspoon freshly ground black pepper

8 thick slices country bread

To make the rouille, grind the chile to a powder using a mortar and pestle. Add the garlic and salt, crushing and pounding until a paste forms. Add the bread crumbs and the saffron with its soaking water and incorporate into the paste. Scrape the paste into a medium bowl. Add the egg yolks and whisk until the mixture has thickened. Whisking constantly, slowly add the olive oil, a drop at a time, until the mixture emulsifies and a mayonnaise-like consistency forms. Add only as much of the oil as needed to achieve a good consistency. Cover and refrigerate the rouille until serving.

To make the fish stock, warm the olive oil in a Dutch oven or small stockpot over medium-high heat. When it is hot, add the onion, garlic, carrots, and the white part of the leek and sauté, stirring, until limp, 2 to 3 minutes. Add the fish heads and cook, stirring, until they begin to turn opaque, about 3 minutes. Add the leek greens, the parsley, thyme, peppercorns, wine, and 6 to 8 cups water and bring to a boil. Skim off any foam that rises to the surface with a slotted spoon. Decrease the heat to low, cover, and simmer for about 30 minutes.

Remove from the heat. Using a slotted spoon or wire skimmer, remove and discard the large solids, then strain the stock through a chinois or a colander lined with cheesecloth. Use immediately, or let cool, cover, and refrigerate for up to 1 day or freeze for up to 3 months.

To make the soup, warm 4 tablespoons of the olive oil in a soup pot over medium heat. Add the fish, 2 garlic cloves, and the onions. Cook, stirring, until the fish begin to change color and fall apart. Add the potatoes, bay leaves, and thyme and continue cooking, stirring to prevent burning, about 5 minutes. Stir in the tomatoes. Add 2 cups of the stock and scrape up any bits. Add the remaining 2 cups of stock, 1 cup water, the fennel, salt, and pepper. Cover and cook over low heat until the potatoes are tender, about 30 minutes.

Position a food mill over a bowl. Pour the contents of the soup pot into the mill and purée. Discard the debris in the mill. Rinse the mill thoroughly and repeat. Transfer to a large saucepan and set aside.

Preheat the oven to 350°F. Drizzle the bread with the remaining 2 tablespoons of olive oil and toast until just barely golden. Remove and rub with garlic. To serve, ladle the soup into bowls, top with a teaspoon of rouille and a slice of toast alongside.

serves 8

Le Grand Aïoli
Aïoli with Vegetables and Salted Cod

Every summer, for the fifteenth of August, Fox-Amphoux, the village where my brother and I grew up, hosts a village feast, a Grand Aïoli, a party that lasts for days, culminating on the last day with the feast and *pétanque* (French bocce ball) tournament. The feast itself consists of platters of boiled vegetables, refreshed salted cod, and bowls of homemade aïoli, all cooked by the women and men of the village. The days preceding are filled with the first rounds of the pétanque competition, lots and lots of pastis and rosé wine, and in the evenings very eclectic, if not somewhat embarrassing, DJs or rock bands. As kids we would dress up a bit in party clothes. I remember sporting my skinny-leg Gloria Vanderbilt yellow cords, wedge espadrilles, and possibly a side ponytail, then dancing away with my girlfriends to Abba, the Bee Gees, and Donna Summer. Too young for drinking or boys, the evening fun usually included spying on Aileen's older brother and his friends, strange and curious teenagers; the girls all smoked and wore lightweight cotton scarves, a look I still find undeniably French. —Ethel

6 pieces salted cod, 4 to 5 ounces each

3 cloves garlic, peeled and crushed

1 teaspoon coarse sea salt

¼ teaspoon freshly ground black pepper

2 egg yolks

1½ cups extra-virgin olive oil

12 boiling potatoes, such as White Rose or Yellow Finn, peels intact

12 medium-size carrots, peeled

1 pound haricots verts or other small green beans, stem ends removed

6 eggs

To refresh the cod, rinse it well in water, then place it in a large bowl, cover with water, and let it soak for 6 to 8 hours, changing the water every 2 hours. To test, bring a small pan of water to a simmer over low heat, drop in a 1-inch piece of the rinsed fish, cook for 3 to 4 minutes, remove, and taste. It should be pleasantly salted and edible. If still too salty, continue soaking for several more hours.

In a small bowl, crush together the garlic and salt using a wooden spoon. In a larger bowl, lightly beat the egg yolks. Very slowly drizzle in the olive oil, a teaspoon at a time, into the yolks, whisking constantly. Continue this slow process until all the oil is incorporated and an emulsion has formed. Aïoli is finicky and sometimes it just doesn't set; if this happens, try again. Once the mayonnaise has formed, stir in the garlic mixture and the black pepper. Refrigerate until ready to serve.

Bring a large pot of water to a boil. Add the potatoes and cook until easily pierced with a fork, about 20 minutes. Using a slotted spoon, remove them from the water and set aside on a platter.

Using the same water, cook the carrots until they are tender but still firm, about 15 minutes. They too should easily be pierced with a fork. Using a slotted spoon, remove from the water and set aside on the platter.

Continue the process for cooking the green beans, but just cook for 5 minutes. Drain the beans and rinse them with cold water to stop the cooking process. Pat dry and transfer to the platter of vegetables.

Place the eggs in a pot of water, bring the water to a boil, turn off the heat, and let the eggs sit in the hot water for 10 minutes. Drain the water from the pot and run cold water over the eggs for about 3 minutes. Remove the eggs, let cool, and peel. Cut the eggs in half lengthwise and arrange on the platter.

To cook the fish, bring a large skillet of water to a simmer. Poach the cod fillets until they gently flake apart, 5 to 6 minutes. Remove from the skillet and pat dry.

To serve, arrange the vegetables, eggs, and fish on a large platter and put the aïoli in several bowls on the table.

serves 6

BROUILLADE AUX TRUFFES
Truffled Eggs

We didn't spend many winters in France, only a few when we lived there, and then again once or twice in my twenties when I did have a very cloak-and-dagger experience at a truffle market. Before the dark winter skies settled, my mom and I headed to the market (held in the same square as the weekly vegetable market) with Serge, an old family friend. Truffles can sell for hundreds of dollars a pound and the parking lot was filled with expensive black cars from Nice, Monaco, and even Italy. People walked from trunk to trunk of each car, shrouding their transactions behind one another, no checks, just wads of cash exchanging hands. It was a very quiet, male-dominated scene. Later as we settled into the café for a coffee (I was of this age now!), people were starting to drink and put their multi-hundred-dollar purchases on the table to admire.

—Ethel

8 eggs, lightly beaten

½ ounce black truffle, shaved (substitute 1 teaspoon truffle oil)

6 tablespoons unsalted butter, at room temperature

¾ teaspoon coarse sea salt

½ teaspoon freshly ground white pepper

4 thick slices brioche, lightly toasted

In the bottom of a double boiler, heat water to a simmer. Add the eggs and truffle to the top pan of the double boiler and whisk together. Add the butter, salt, and white pepper and continue whisking gently until small curds begin to form, resembling cottage cheese. Remove from the heat, and serve immediately while hot, alongside the brioche toast.

serves 4

MELON AU JAMBON CRU
Prosciutto-Wrapped Melon

I first saw this on a stark white plate under bad lighting next to rows and rows of other melon slices wrapped in saggy ham. This not-so-well-thought-out presentation could always be found at the Casino grocery store cafeteria, a chain location to eat in any city we were visiting, always inexpensive most likely, at best mediocre. It was the first time I saw melon wrapped in ham, which I thought was strange and hilarious. I passed it by with my plastic red lunch tray, ready to pick something familiar like chicken, and didn't see this dish again until we had it at a close family friend's house. That time it was gorgeous: a beautiful, pink, thin blanket of marbled ham wrapped around a blush/light orange melon. The sweet and salty combination married so well, I completely forgot about the unimpressive Casino version.

—Sara

1 small ripe cantaloupe, a French
    Charantais if possible

8 thin slices prosciutto

To prepare the melon, slice it in half lengthwise from the stem end. Use a large spoon to scoop the seeds from the center. Cut each half of the melon into 4 slices and remove the rind from each. Take a slice of prosciutto from the short end and wrap it around the center of a slice of melon. Continue until all the slices are wrapped. Transfer to the refrigerator until ready to serve.

serves 4 to 8

LAPIN AUX CAROTTES, OIGNONS, ET POMMES DE TERRE
Braised Rabbit with Carrots, Onions, and Potatoes

We often had fresh game for dinner at a friend of my dad's, Dr. Guillemin. My sister and I loved Dr. Guillemin's house because he had such a huge amount of land; you could have four or five full-field soccer games going on at once in his backyard. He also had many grandkids and built a two-story playhouse for them, complete with a kitchen and play utensils, small beds with flower linens, and mini tables and chairs. Marius, his caretaker, would often hunt for rabbit on their property the day before our feast, ready with a fresh kill when we arrived that afternoon. For whatever reason, dead game, no matter how cute or fluffy it was, didn't faze me as a kid—I was excited to eat something that I could see prepped from start to finish. I remember the way the big wooden table in the kitchen looked from my eye level, as if I were in the front row seat of animal open-heart surgery: mini kidneys here, tiny heart there, and a floppy soft rabbit jacket. I wanted to poke all the organs with disgusted fascination, not realizing that everything on that table was edible. At dinnertime, we were often picking out the buckshot while we ate the rabbit meat, trying to be discreet and polite, spitting it out in our napkins with a smile.

—Sara

3 tablespoons extra-virgin olive oil

3 cloves garlic, peeled and coarsely chopped

1 medium yellow onion, peeled and cut into
    2- by ½-inch pieces

1 rabbit (about 3 pounds), cut into pieces
    (ask your butcher), innards discarded

5 sprigs fresh thyme

2 fresh or dried bay leaves

1 teaspoon coarse sea salt

½ teaspoon freshly ground black pepper

2 cups white wine

2 tablespoons unsalted butter

4 medium carrots, peeled and cut into
    1-inch pieces

8 to 10 new potatoes, such as Yukon Gold,
    Yellow Finn, or White Rose, peeled

One 28-ounce can crushed tomatoes

Warm the olive oil in the bottom of a Dutch oven or stockpot over medium heat. Add the garlic and onion, and cook until fragrant and the onion is translucent, about 5 minutes. Add the rabbit pieces, the thyme, bay leaves, salt, and pepper. Cook for about 5 minutes, browning the rabbit. Add the wine and deglaze the pot, scraping the browned bits from the bottom

and sides. Stir in the butter, then add the carrots, potatoes, and tomatoes. Add enough water to just cover the meat. Bring the braising liquid to a slow simmer, making sure it doesn't boil. Decrease the heat to low and cook, uncovered, for 1½ hours. Test the meat for doneness with a fork. The fork should easily pierce the meat, which should then fall from the bone without resistance. If the meat appears tough, continue to cook until it is fork-tender and easily flakes when pierced with a fork.

Remove the rabbit meat from the pot, place on a serving dish, and spoon about ½ cup of the liquid over the meat. Cover with aluminum foil and set aside. Increase the heat for the braising liquid to medium and cook, uncovered, stirring gently, until it reduces by one-quarter, about 15 minutes. Pour the braising liquid and vegetables over the meat and serve.

serves 6

ESCARGOTS
Snails in Garlic Butter

Summer rainstorms filled the skies with wild flashes of lightning and shattering cracks of thunder, but when the storm passed, especially in the evening, out came the flashlights and the kids. Yes, we four- to eight-year-olds hopped on the hood of the truck of our friend and neighbor Pascal, the lights went on, and we trolled down the winding, single-lane road hunting for snails. The bigger the better, and once they were collected they were plopped into wire baskets with lids. We headed to the rocky roadside to tear handfuls of pungent wild thyme for snail feeding. The baskets were filled with thyme and the snails left to cleanse, their meat being seasoned by the diet of wild thyme. Two weeks later, they were boiled up in a seasoned broth of bay, thyme, salt, and garlic, tucked back into snail shells, stuffed with garlic butter, and then broiled. Now, whenever we eat snails we get them canned from specialty gourmet shops or online, or from France in suitcases.

—Ethel

24 canned snails (escargots de Bourgogne)

24 snail shells

8 tablespoons butter

¼ cup finely chopped Italian
    flat-leaf parsley

3 cloves garlic, peeled and finely chopped

1 teaspoon sea salt

1 baguette, cut into ½-inch slices

Preheat the broiler.

Drain and rinse the snails, pat dry, and tuck deep into the shells.

In a mixing bowl, cream together the butter, parsley, garlic, and salt. Spoon a generous teaspoon of the butter mixture into each shell and press firmly in to seal the shell, as hot air can build up inside and send hot snails flying. Place the snails in a baking dish, openings facing upward so the melted butter doesn't drain out.

Place the snails under the broiler and cook until the butter is melted, 3 to 5 minutes. Serve hot with the baguette.

serves 4

BOUCHÉES À LA REINE
Puff Pastry Shells Filled with Chanterelles and Chicken

One of my dad's friends owned a house outside of Lyon. He had a gardener/cook, who had a lovely round wife, both of whom lived with him on the premises. They were so adorable, short and stocky, ready to show us the most beautiful ingredients they were preparing for dinner. There was a year that must have been extremely wet because during one of our visits the cook pulled out a huge brown basket full of the most perfect golden chanterelles. At the time, I had no idea what they were and how coveted they were, but by the looks of them and how everyone else reacted to the bounty, I knew they were special. They brought a taste of the woods to the plate, and I thought of the trees we had just been climbing outside. The chanterelles had brought the outside in.

—Sara

2 tablespoons olive oil

2 tablespoons finely chopped shallot

1 (5- to 6-ounce) boneless, skinless chicken
    breast, cut into ½-inch cubes

2 cups chanterelle mushrooms, rinsed and
    coarsely chopped

1 teaspoon fresh thyme leaves

½ cup white wine

4 tablespoons unsalted butter

3 tablespoons all-purpose flour

½ cup chicken stock

1 cup whole milk

6 frozen puff pastry shells, 3½ inches or so
    in diameter

Salt and pepper

Preheat the oven to 350°F.

Warm the olive oil in a large skillet over medium heat. Add the shallot and sauté, stirring often with a wooden spoon, until fragrant and just translucent, about 2 minutes.

Increase the heat to medium high. Add the chicken, cook until lightly browned on all sides, about 5 minutes. Add the mushrooms, thyme, and white wine. Cook for 2 minutes, using the spoon to scrape the caramelized bits of shallot, chicken, and mushrooms from the bottom and sides of the pan. Add the butter and stir until melted; decrease the heat to low. Sprinkle the flour over the top and stir to create a roux. Add in the chicken stock, stirring constantly, then pour in the milk. Increase the heat to medium high and bring to a simmer. The sauce will begin to thicken, so remove it from the heat when it sticks easily to the back of the spoon, 5 to 7 minutes. Taste and adjust the seasoning with more salt and pepper as needed.

While you bake the shells, let mixture stand in the hot pan to allow the sauce to thicken.

Bake the puff pastry shells according to the package directions. Remove from the oven, fill with the mushroom and chicken filling, and return to the oven. Bake for another 10 minutes, until heated through, and serve immediately.

serves 8

DAUBE
Beef Stew

Boeuf bourguignon, *coq au vin*, *daube*, and *cassoulet* are stews with elegant names that all share wine as an ingredient. I loved when my mom cooked French stew wherever we were living. Usually for us, they were meals for a special occasion, mostly birthdays. We always brought home from Europe secret stashes of dried herbs we picked from the hillsides and cheeses we had bought the day before leaving, which may not have been allowed by U.S. customs. But I have no memory of us ever being caught, and, besides, the ingredients were essential to tide us over flavorwise until the following year.

—Ethel

4 pounds boneless beef chuck roast or a combination of boneless chuck and shank

2 medium yellow onions, 1 quartered, 1 diced

3 carrots

8 sprigs fresh thyme

3 fresh bay leaves

1 sprig rosemary, about 6 inches long

2 teaspoons sea salt

1 tablespoon freshly ground black pepper

4 cloves garlic

1 orange zest strip, 4 inches long and ½ inch wide

1 bottle dry red wine

½ cup minced pancetta

2 tablespoons all-purpose flour

2 ounces or so sliced dried cèpes or porcini mushrooms, some broken, some whole, soaked in 1 cup boiling water for 30 minutes

½ cup chopped fresh Italian flat-leaf parsley

Cut the meat into 2½-inch cubes. Trim and discard any large pieces of fat. Place the meat in a large bowl. Add the quartered onion along with the carrots, thyme, bay leaves, rosemary,

1 teaspoon salt, ½ tablespoon pepper, 2 cloves garlic, and the orange zest. Pour the wine over and turn all to mix well. Cover and let marinate overnight.

Render the pancetta in a heavy-bottomed stockpot or Dutch oven over medium heat. You should have about ¼ cup fat. If not, add a mix of butter and olive oil to make up the difference. Increase the heat to medium-high and add the diced onion. Mince the remaining 2 cloves of garlic and add. Sauté in the fat, then remove the pancetta to a plate.

Remove the meat from the marinade, reserving the marinade. Drain the meat and pat it very dry with paper towels or a clean dry dishcloth. Sauté a few pieces at a time, turning to brown well and removing each batch to a bowl. After the last one, add the flour and cook until it browns a bit, but be careful not to burn it.

Raise the heat to high and slowly pour in the reserved marinade, stirring and scraping to loosen any clinging bits. Return the sautéed onions, garlic, and the meat to the pot, along with any collected juices.

Add the remaining 1 teaspoon salt and ½ tablespoon pepper and 1 cup water. Bring to a boil, then decrease the heat to low, cover, and simmer until the meat can be cut with a fork. During the last half hour of cooking, add the soaked mushrooms. Drain their soaking water in a fine-mesh sieve, then add the soaking water to the stew as well.

Remove from the heat. Discard the herb stems and quartered onion. Skim off any excess fat, if desired. Serve hot, garnished with the parsley and accompanied by egg noodles, mashed potatoes, or polenta.

serves 6 to 8

RÔTI DE PORC ET SAUCE AUX CÈPES
Roast Pork Loin with Rosemary and Porcini Mushrooms

We had pig, a very, very large pig, and her name was Lucretia. She was friendly and always seemed to have a dozen squeaky little piglets running underfoot. My father and I would take the goats out into the woods for the day and Lucretia would sometimes join us. My father carried a long stick, which he used to nudge and guide her, so I suppose we used to take our pig for walks. So many little piglets meant lots of pork meals. Although most of the piglets were sold off to friends and neighbors, at least one was kept for us, soon to become pork chops, *lardon* (pancetta), and salted hams and roasts.

—Ethel

3-pound pork loin roast (ask your butcher to tie)

2 teaspoons coarse sea salt

½ teaspoon freshly ground black pepper

2 tablespoons extra-virgin olive oil

½ cup (1 stick) unsalted butter

1 ounce dried *cèpes* (porcini) mushrooms

4 sprigs fresh rosemary, each 4 to 6 inches long

3 cloves garlic, peeled and crushed

Preheat the oven to 350°F.

Rub the roast all over with the salt and pepper. In a large ovenproof skillet, warm the olive oil over medium heat Add the roast and brown, letting the meat sear for 1 to 2 minutes on each side, including the ends before turning.

In a small saucepan over low heat, melt the butter, then add the dried mushrooms, rosemary, and garlic. Simmer for 10 to 15 minutes, stirring occasionally, until fragrant and the mushrooms begin to soften. Position the roast in the large skillet with the fat facing upward, baste the roast with the seasoned butter, and add a few of the mushrooms and rosemary sprigs from the sauce to the pan. Transfer the pork to the oven and baste every 10 to 15 minutes with the butter sauce, adding all the remaining mushrooms and rosemary from the sauce after 20 minutes.

Cook the roast until an internal meat thermometer reads 145°F at the thickest part, about 1 hour. Remove from the oven, tent with a piece of foil, and let rest for 10 to 15 minutes. Cut ½-inch-thick slices and serve, topping with the pan juices and mushrooms from the pan.

serves 8 to 10

GNOCCHI À LA BOLOGNAISE
Potato Dumplings with Bolognese Sauce

Marie's mother, Mémé Scifino, lived with them and mostly spoke an Italian dialect mingled with a bit of French. I never understood much of what she said to me, but she gave me treats, wore beautiful gold jewelry, spent her days cooking tomato sauce, polenta, pickled mushrooms, lasagna, and plump potato dumplings called gnocchi. Some days we were invited over for lunch, and on these days the courses were infinite: first charcuterie, then braised artichokes and ratatouille, then pasta or gnocchi with Bolognese sauce, next the meat, roasted pork or lamb chops, then salad, next cheese, and finally at least one dessert. Every year I would forget that I would be full by the time the meat came, and our whole family forgot the golden rule, which was to refuse seconds.

—Ethel

BOLOGNESE SAUCE

½ cup heavy cream

10 ounces pancetta, diced

1 cup finely chopped carrots

¾ cup finely chopped celery

1 cup finely chopped yellow onion

1 teaspoon coarse sea salt

½ teaspoon freshly ground black pepper

¾ pound ground chuck

½ pound ground veal

½ cup dry white wine

4 cloves garlic, peeled and minced

2 tablespoons tomato paste diluted in
    ¼ cup water

½ cup beef stock

1 cup whole milk

In a small saucepan, bring the cream to a simmer over medium heat and then reduce it by one-third. About 6 tablespoons of cream should remain. Remove from the heat.

In a large saucepan, render the pancetta over medium heat, about 8 minutes, or until almost all the fat is rendered. Stir in the carrots, celery, and onion. Stir in ½ teaspoon salt and ¼ teaspoon pepper. Sauté the vegetables for about 3 minutes, or until they are translucent.

In a mixing bowl, combine the ground meats. Season the meats lightly with salt and pepper. Increase the heat and stir the meat into the vegetables. Brown the meat for 5 minutes, or until the meat is medium brown in color. Stir in the wine, garlic, diluted tomato paste, and beef stock and decrease the heat to very low. Cook, partially covered, for 2 hours. Every 15 to

20 minutes stir in a tablespoon or so of the milk until it has all been incorporated. Stir in the reduced cream. Season with the remaining salt and pepper and set aside until ready to serve.

GNOCCHI

2½ pounds russet potatoes, washed

1 egg

1 cup all-purpose flour, plus more for
   coating

½ teaspoon salt

½ cup grated Parmesan cheese

Boil the potatoes in water until tender all the way through, 20 to 25 minutes. While they are still hot, peel and pass them through a vegetable mill or grate them on the large hole of a handheld grater into a bowl. Add the egg and flour, mixing well. Knead on a floured board until the dough is soft and sticky. Take 1 cup of the dough at a time, and with the palms of your hands, roll it into a cylinder 1 foot long. Cut it in half and roll each of the 2 pieces into a 12-inch cylinder. Cut into ½-inch pieces and coat thoroughly with flour.

Bring a large pot of salted water to a boil and cook 2 dozen or so gnocchi at a time until they float to the surface, which takes only moments.

Using a slotted spoon, transfer the gnocchi to a shallow serving bowl or platter and ladle about half of the Bolognese sauce on top. Serve the rest of the sauce separately in a small bowl. Place the cheese in a small bowl on the table.

serves 8

ÎLES FLOTTANTES
Poached Meringues in Crème Anglaise

This was a dessert my mom often made for my dad when they were newlyweds. It's a funny dish, a playful one, and it was really difficult for my mom to achieve custard that was thick and not soupy. I imagine her and my dad in their tiny kitchen in their tiny Paris apartment, young and in love, my mom getting frustrated at how the custard wasn't thickening, and my dad laughing, being playful, and not caring. Eventually, after a few glasses of wine and a few attempts at making the dish, my mom probably got distracted, they turned on some Edith Piaf (specifically "Non, Je Ne Regrette Rien") and danced around the apartment. It was a perfect reminder to not be so hard on yourself in the kitchen and enjoy the simple things in life.

—Sara

CRÈME ANGLAISE

1½ cups half-and-half

1 (2-inch) long vanilla bean, sliced
    lengthwise

4 egg yolks

⅓ cup sugar

Warm the half-and-half and the vanilla bean in a small saucepan over medium heat until tiny bubbles form at the sides. Make sure it doesn't boil.

In a medium mixing bowl, whisk together the egg yolks and sugar until smooth.

Remove the vanilla bean from the hot half-and-half and slowly pour about ½ cup of the hot cream into the egg mixture, whisking until well blended. Slowly pour the egg mixture back into the saucepan with the remaining hot cream, whisking constantly. Return the crème anglaise to medium-low heat, whisking constantly, and continue to cook until the cream thickens and coats the back of the spoon, about 3 minutes. Transfer to a bowl, press a piece of plastic wrap against the top of the cream, and chill completely.

MERINGUES

8 egg whites

¾ cup sugar

½ teaspoon salt

Whisk the egg whites in the bowl of a stand mixer fitted with the whisk attachment or in a large mixing bowl using a hand mixer until they are very stiff. Add the sugar and salt, a little at a time.

Bring a large saucepan of water to a boil and reduce to a simmer. The trick for perfect floating islands meringue is the gentle poaching. Using a large serving spoon, scoop a ½-cup mound of the meringue and gently lower into the simmering water. The meringue will slip from the spoon once it is submerged. Working in batches of 2 to 3, poach the mounds for 4 to 5 minutes. Gently lift them from the water and set onto a tray or large platter.

To serve, ladle a ¼ to ⅓ cup of crème anglaise into individual shallow bowls and place an island of poached meringue in the middle. Serve immediately.

serves 8

ROSES DES SABLES
Chocolate Cornflake Treats

"What do you want for breakfast, Sara—cornflakes?" I can hear my dad's friend's voice (Michel) ask me with such sweetness and quick determination in part French, part broken English. Maybe it was the comfort of seeing the logo as I did in the States (the bright red and green rooster). It brought a little bit of home to the French table and somehow took the strangeness away from the boxed milk. *Roses des Sables* is a playful dessert, combining one of the oldest cereals in America with rich French chocolate. I always wanted each of the pieces to last as long as they could, so instead of chomping down on the treats right away, I would let the chocolate dissolve on my tongue and down my throat until I was left with nothing but a little pocket of crunchy cereal.

—Sara

4 cups unsweetened cornflakes

6 ounces dark chocolate

½ cup salted butter

3 tablespoons powdered sugar

Line a baking sheet with parchment paper or set out forty small paper candy papers, 1-ounce size. Place the cornflakes into a large mixing bowl.

Fill the bottom of a double boiler with water and bring to a boil. Add the chocolate and butter to the top pan and melt together, stirring until smooth. Stir in the powdered sugar and mix until smooth.

Pour the chocolate mixture over the cornflakes and using a rubber spatula, gently fold the cornflakes and chocolate together to coat. Spoon the mixture, 1 teaspoon at a time, onto the baking sheet or into the paper candy cups. Let harden, about 40 minutes.

makes 40

METRIC CONVERSIONS AND EQUIVALENTS

TO CONVERT / MULTIPLY

TO CONVERT	MULTIPLY
Ounces to grams	Ounces by 28.35
Pounds to kilograms	Pounds by .454
Teaspoons to milliliters	Teaspoons by 4.93
Tablespoons to milliliters	Tablespoons by 14.79
Fluid ounces to milliliters	Fluid ounces by 29.57
Cups to milliliters	Cups by 236.59
Cups to liters	Cups by .236
Pints to liters	Pints by .473
Quarts to liters	Quarts by .946
Gallons to liters	Gallons by 3.785
Inches to centimeters	Inches by 2.54

APPROXIMATE METRIC EQUIVALENTS
VOLUME

¼ teaspoon	1 milliliter
½ teaspoon	2.5 milliliters
¾ teaspoon	4 milliliters
1 teaspoon	5 milliliters
1¼ teaspoons	6 milliliters
1½ teaspoons	7.5 milliliters
1¾ teaspoons	8.5 milliliters
2 teaspoons	10 milliliters
1 tablespoon (½ fluid ounce)	15 milliliters
2 tablespoons (1 fluid ounce)	30 milliliters
¼ cup	60 milliliters
⅓ cup	80 milliliters
½ cup (4 fluid ounces)	120 milliliters
⅔ cup	160 milliliters
¾ cup	180 milliliters
1 cup (8 fluid ounces)	240 milliliters
1¼ cups	300 milliliters
1½ cups (12 fluid ounces)	360 milliliters
1⅔ cups	400 milliliters
2 cups (1 pint)	460 milliliters
3 cups	700 milliliters
4 cups (1 quart)	0.95 liter
1 quart plus ¼ cup	1 liter
4 quarts (1 gallon)	3.8 liters

WEIGHT

¼ ounce	7 grams
½ ounce	14 grams
¾ ounce	21 grams
1 ounce	28 grams
1¼ ounces	35 grams
1½ ounces	42.5 grams
1⅔ ounces	45 grams
2 ounces	57 grams
3 ounces	85 grams
4 ounces (¼ pound)	113 grams
5 ounces	142 grams
6 ounces	170 grams
7 ounces	198 grams
8 ounces (½ pound)	227 grams
16 ounces (1 pound)	454 grams
35.25 ounces (2.2 pounds)	1 kilogram

LENGTH

⅛ inch	3 millimeters
¼ inch	6 millimeters
½ inch	1¼ centimeters
1 inch	2½ centimeters
2 inches	5 centimeters
2½ inches	6 centimeters
4 inches	10 centimeters
5 inches	13 centimeters
6 inches	15¼ centimeters
12 inches (1 foot)	30 centimeters

OVEN TEMPERATURES

To convert Fahrenheit to Celsius, subtract 32 from Fahrenheit, multiply the result by 5, then divide by 9.

DESCRIPTION	FAHRENHEIT	CELSIUS	BRITISH GAS MARK
Very cool	200°	95°	0
Very cool	225°	110°	¼
Very cool	250°	120°	½
Cool	275°	135°	1
Cool	300°	150°	2
Warm	325°	165°	3
Moderate	350°	175°	4
Moderately hot	375°	190°	5
Fairly hot	400°	200°	6
Hot	425°	220°	7
Very hot	450°	230°	8
Very hot	475°	245°	9

COMMON INGREDIENTS AND THEIR APPROXIMATE EQUIVALENTS

1 cup uncooked white rice = 185 grams

1 cup all-purpose flour = 140 grams

1 stick butter (4 ounces • ½ cup • 8 tablespoons) = 110 grams

1 cup butter (8 ounces • 2 sticks • 16 tablespoons) = 220 grams

1 cup brown sugar, firmly packed = 225 grams

1 cup granulated sugar = 200 grams

Information compiled from a variety of sources, including *Recipes into Type* by Joan Whitman and Dolores Simon (Newton, MA: Biscuit Books, 2000); *The New Food Lover's Companion* by Sharon Tyler Herbst (Hauppauge, NY: Barron's, 1995); and *Rosemary Brown's Big Kitchen Instruction Book* (Kansas City, MO: Andrews McMeel, 1998).

ACKNOWLEDGMENTS

Thank you to my husband, Laurent, who supports me with enthusiasm at every turn. I must thank my children, Oscar and Raphael, who are equally as enthusiastic as their father and whose faces grace the pages of this book, their childhood summers echoing my own. Thank you to my mother and father, Georgeanne Brennan and Donald Brennan, who carted me around the world throughout my childhood. And to my brother, Oliver Brennan, who shared so many crazy adventures with me during those childhood years. Thank you to my stepfather, Jim Schrupp, who first read this manuscript with a loving and critical eye. Thank you to my dear friend and co-author, Sara Remington, whose talent and creativity inspires me in countless ways.

—Ethel

Thank you to my sister, Jennifer Remington, who fondly shares my French memories, which wouldn't be the same without her. I'm so happy I had a partner in these adventures; nothing can replace the sisterly fun, laughter, long drives, and car fights. To Dan Fisher, my life love, my future husband. Thank you for always giving me the support and laughter that I need, and loving me for who I am and what I do. I adore you.

Thank you to Ethel Brennan; I couldn't ask for a better writing partner and friend throughout this whole process. Not only were you so much fun to be around, but your energy, initiative, and drive were inspiring. Your knowledge and talent is incredible. And you're a supermom. You get things DONE.

Very deepest thanks to Georgeanne Brennan, as this book would not exist without you either. You mean to Ethel what my parents mean to me, and you created a beautiful, colorful, delicious life for your family in France. Your help and guidance with the recipes and memories was invaluable, and you so generously opened your doors to me in France with endless positive thinking, and a special thanks to your husband, Jim Schrupp, who meticulously read over our manuscript, our first copy editor.

A big thank-you to Steve Block, who gave me wonderful support with my film processing—something that is becoming a lost art. A very special thank-you to my friends Gia Canali, Matt McManus, and Tom Santosusso, I love you guys! You were all so supportive throughout this process, and thank you for lending me some of the best, drool-worthy cameras I have laid my eyes and hands on, specifically that pass-out-gorgeous M6 Leica with the 50mm f1 lens.

Lastly, thank you, thank you, thank you to all the French family friends of my parents, who opened their homes to us Remingtons throughout our summertime journeys. Not only did you feed us with endless, delicious, memorable food, but you also fed our hearts and minds with beautiful history, art, music, and culture. We forever thank you.

—Sara

Thank you to our editor, Jean Lucas, who seemingly let us go wild creatively. We felt supported from the moment we submitted our proposal and are honored to have had the opportunity to write and photograph this very personal culinary biography of our childhoods. Thank you to our publisher, Kirsty Melville, who took a chance with us, gave us unlimited creative freedom, and believed this very personal story was something worth investing in. Thank you to Laurent, who watched the boys while we worked, supporting us all the way. A special thank-you to all the kids we photographed: Oscar and Raphael Rigobert, Marion and Fiona Krauze, Lucie Gayde, Julien Durango, Hugo Kleiman, Oona Grace and Sidney Brennan. Thank you to all of the friends and family who opened their homes to us: Sylvie Kleiman-Lafon, whose Paris kitchen is on the cover; to Ethel's in-laws, Paulette and Raymond Rigobert, who took such good care of us during our days of photography, both in Paris and Provence; to Laurent's sister Fabienne Krauze for helping us find locations in the streets of Paris; to Joanne Kaufman and Jim Gutensohn, and Georgina and Deny Fines, for sharing their family homes with us; and to Adèle and Pascal Degremont for joining in the fun. We would like to thank the lovely Anne Deregnaucourt for her Rose de Sables; Marie Palazolli for her gnocchi; her daughter Aileen Palazolli and Roberto for tiramisu; Luc Chaffard for early morning coffee, croissants, and goat herding along the rocky hills of Haute Provence; and to Jean and Chantal Serre, and Josianne Serre, for allowing us to photograph their restaurant and epicerie. Thank you Abby Stolfo, who tested recipes for us at crucial moment during the writing process.

Thank you to Francesca Bautista and Imelda Picherit, our beloved designer and photo editor; we knew from the very beginning that we needed you both to go forward with our vision, or our shared vision as the case may be. Francesca, you are an extraordinary talent, and we are so lucky to have you as a friend, colleague, and collaborator. Bisou to Tristan. We must also thank your very talented mother, Jackie Bautista, who helped us strengthen and clarify our written story.

—Ethel & Sara

INDEX